# ROTTENOMICS

## REPLACING ECONOMICS

## DAVID E BLAND

# CONTENTS

# INTRODUCTION

A few months ago I published an e-book under the title *Sinking Britain.* In it, I mistakenly tried to run together an account of how and why Britain got into the present economic crisis [and to show how deep that crisis is] with my analysis of why Economics itself is a dangerously fallacious subject. It made for a dense, even impenetrable text that deservedly failed to attract the attention that I had hoped to gain. I have spent several months separating out the two strands and in this small volume I present the principles on which a rational understanding of the economy can be based.

A slimmed-down sister text, an expurgated *Sinking Britain* is also available.

I hope that this book will benefit my fellow-citizens who share a widespread perplexity at the state of our economic affairs and at the egotistical incompetence with which politicians repeatedly fail adequately to address these issues.

# FIRST PRINCIPLES

Democratic politics is increasingly confronted by a lack of confidence in both institutions and politicians, as governments fail to address both global and local issues to the satisfaction of the people who have the right to vote in elections. So great is that lack of confidence, especially in Europe and particularly in the UK that an increasing percentage of the population are staying away from elections; or are supporting 'fringe parties' that seek to disrupt the prevailing consensus. In several of the long-established democracies there is a gulf between a self-selected 'political class' and the growing majority who have no wish to engage in activities which they see as deceitful, self-serving and frequently perverse. The polarisation of Republicans and Democrats in the USA has been destructive for several years and shows no sign of improvement. In some countries politics is seen as a means of enriching politicians and bureaucrats through bribes, by the sale of state assets and of licences to extract natural resources, and by allowing firms to market unsafe or inadequate products; as well as making it possible to buy decisions in the courts. Even in the countries where the law and the force of public opinion are sufficiently strong to retain public confidence in the overall integrity of the legal system, political expediency increasingly challenges the absolute maintenance of standards in public life.

A major area for concern is the gap between the economic policy that governments impose, usually at the instance of economic advisers, and the aspirations of the mass of the population. The starting-point for this book is to challenge the legitimacy of academic Economics as an explanation of how wealth is made and circulated by human beings. Economics does not explain what wealth is, or how people aspire to it. Given that the subject fails in that basic sense, it is useless as a guide to policy. Politics and the management of the economy are inseparable. The fundamental failing of formal Economics is that it is based on a 'pure' politics-free *model* of the ideal transaction – an act of exchange between a seller and a buyer – which is deployed as a template for assessing the effectiveness and efficiency of any economic process or event. Economists assert that human welfare is optimised by maximising the proportion of transactions in an economy that are unregulated by the state.

What the inventors of Economics called a 'perfect' transaction takes place in an imaginary [normative] world: the parties to the event are in effect disembodied intellects which are liberated from any real-world contextual pressure. This is refined nonsense. Every economic event follows from a decision that is taken by a living human person acting on his or her own responsibility, or on behalf of an entity that is empowered to act as a 'legal person': such as a company, a government agency or a voluntary organisation. Every natural or legal person is an entity that can create, acquire, retain, sell, give, use, damage, destroy, absorb or excrete commodities and services. Every person who ever lived has beliefs, likes and dislikes, lusts and feelings of altruism; and is subject to the need for air, water, food and a secure resting-place. Provided that the rational rule of law is in force, every recognised person can own both material things and immaterial assets [such as shares in companies, bank deposits and intellectual property] over long periods of time. Individuals and organisations make contracts that create liabilities to other organisations and individuals, which the counterparties can regard as their assets; and they can receive contractual promises from other individuals and organisations which they can treat as their assets. Every economic person needs to maintain itself while and after any transaction is being made: individuals need subsistence, and to get a living they must earn wages, receive fees, take profits, receive pensions or insurance settlements, or draw money from the state in the forms of pensions and benefits. No transaction takes place in a disembodied dream world: the human individuals involved are moving further away from the last meal, and need the next meal to become available to maintain their life; and firms constantly need income [or to draw on savings, that must in due course be replenished] to maintain their existence. The need for material human subsistence applies as much to the individuals who are responsible for all contracts that cover sophisticated betting and transactions in cyberspace as it does to cash and barter deals in street markets

While Economics is based on a theory of transactions, the much older science of Political Economy – which this book seeks to update and re-establish – teaches that the components of the economy depend for the legal recognition of their existence [and for their beneficial continuance to serve their purpose] on the efficacy of the state and its courts. These components are-:

1.  human beings, and organisations that possess legal personality: *economic agents,*
2.  the assets and liabilities for which human beings are responsible; including the processes by which assets are processed and transmogrified, and the means by which both material things and concepts are transported or transmitted or exchanged.

Tangible assets exist in the physical environment of the earth; with a possibility that this will be extended within the solar system within the proximate future. In the case of immaterial assets and liabilities the geographical location and the legal system where their creators and their counterparties are located are legally recorded and validated: and those legalities ultimately depend on the power of the state that maintains the legal system to assure enforcement of contracts.

Human decisions set in train events that create and transport and transform and trade and use, and destroy, assets [and liabilities, which are negative assets]. Assets are material and immaterial things and situations that are sufficiently desired by people and by organisations that they are willing to exchange other assets [including natural persons' talents, thoughts and their capacity to work] to gain control of them. For hundreds of years assets have collectively been known as *wealth*, which is the term for all the resources that are available to an individual, or to an organisation, or to the people of a state or of a community of states. Unless the rights and the responsibilities of an economic agent in relation to an asset are clear – and are enforceable at law – there is a probability that the asset will not be maintained properly and will therefore be deployed less efficiently in serving humanity that it could and should be. The wave of vandalism that defaced many European and North American cities with graffiti, forced the closure of public lavatories and made parks into no-go zones, most notably in the nineteen-seventies, emerged with the concept that some economies were so rich that confrontations to protect individual assets were not worth the mental and physical stress that would fall on the low-paid lavatory attendant, park keeper or school caretaker who would have intervened in earlier periods when public assets were seen to represent collective wealth that all members of society had a duty to maintain properly.

During the last third of the twentieth century individuals in the affluent countries were coached by television, films, glossy magazines, lavish advertising and peer pressure to concentrate on their own consumption and on the acquisition of personal assets. The acquisitions continued even when the potential resale prices of many of the assets that they acquired became less than the increment in debt that the owner had incurred to buy them in only a few weeks. At the same time companies in general became more concerned with published financial results than with internal and external social obligations: to an extent that a cosmetic concept of 'corporate social responsibility' was introduced as a novelty that firms took on board only so far as it was considered to enhance their public image. The disparity between boardroom employees' and non-executives' 'compensation' and the remuneration of hourly-paid unskilled staff began to increase. However, during the period 1970-2007 it seemed possible in the richest countries to expand the state's role in the economy as the benefits system [even in the USA] spread through an increasing cohort of non-employed and also provided income supplements to lower-paid 'working families' at the expense of taxpayers, both individual and corporate. Effectively oblivious to the reality of an ever-expanding public sector, Economists, governments and even some 'business leaders' shared the Thatcherite delusion that the economy could be coaxed and bullied to approximate more closely to the Economists' model world. Thus they facilitated the wave of privatisation, and artificially enforced 'competition' in business and industry; and they accepted an expansion of the criteria for acceptability of borrowing that was mortally to weaken the countries [especially in Europe] where the agenda was carried furthest.

Most people spend periods of their adult lives sharing aspects of their economic functionality, especially as consumers, in family and other affinity groups. This interactivity is based predominantly on physical proximity to the other people in the group, but the internet and mobile communications have enabled manifold different types of relationship to form; and many non-domestic affinity groups now transcend the boundaries of states. Households are still the commonest asset-sharing groups, among whom breeding pairs of heterosexuals predominate; but there are several types of group in which the participants pool some of their consumption and some of their assets and liabilities with the others, ranging from the intergenerational family to the frequently-changing occupants of a student house. As the law and social morality have developed, members of affinity and domestic groups necessarily distinguish between:

1. the individual's personal economic activities, assets and obligations, *and*
2. each participating individual's interest in the assets, obligations and activities that are conjoint in their family, household or other group.

Experimental socialistic communities have usually foundered on their failure to understand and to apply this simple principle.

Many non-domestic aggregations of assets and liabilities under shared ownership are formed with specific purposes; such as business partnerships; or when people with similar interests or concerns form social clubs, charitable organisations, religious communities and political movements. Once such collectives are established they can become licensed to exist independently by adopting an appropriate identity, which acquires legal personality that is separate from the individuals who constituted it. The people who are engaged in the functioning of the entity are legally required to differentiate clearly between things that are done for and on behalf of the organisation, and actions that they take in their personal capacity outside the purview of the organisation.

A sophisticated economy is created by individuals operating in and with licensed organisations, each of which is legally capable of constructing around itself an *estate* whose components are conventionally 'valued' according to agreed accounting standards and are listed in a register of assets and liabilities. The constituents of the estate that is owned by a successful company or by a wealthy individual may be located in several countries, under various legal systems; but all assets fall within four discrete categories which have distinct economic properties [or characteristics] that give rise to four fundamentally different pricing systems. Economic agents that own significant assets in the most-desired categories are, in the main, perceived to be richer than agents whose assets are fewer and are in the less-desired categories. The broad outline of this differentiation was recognised by

Political Economists in the eighteenth and nineteenth centuries, but since the nineteen twenties the almost-universal adoption of academic Economics has ignored the existence of the differentiation. This failure largely accounts for the increasing irrelevance of the contemporary academic subject to 'real life'.

The categories of assets are:

## 1. Keyn

Pronounced *'cane'* as in *sugar cane.*

The designation of the **keyn** recognises J M Keynes's unique and original understanding of immaterial assets, as set out especially in his *Treatise on Money [1929]*. The category is comprised of assets that Keynes designated *chartalist*, which are conjured into existence by the human mind and are recognised in law to exist. This category includes property rights, the ownership of land and of other material things; and the term also covers cash and deposits that are created by contracts with banks and other financial institutions; plus bonds, bills, stocks, shares, mortgages, pension entitlements, savings certificates of all kinds, rights under insurance policies, and any other sub-category of financial asset. The category also applies to all the assets that have successfully been designated as *intellectual property*: patents, copyright, trademarks etc. In the period when Keynes was active [1890-1947] commodity futures were closely related to material assets [crops and minerals, including oil]: and both on his personal account and as a bursar of his college Keynes traded largely and successfully in those markets; such investments were only moderately risky if the dealer had great knowledge of real-world commodity markets and an understanding of probability: which Keynes possessed to a very high level. Since Keynes's time, a vastly expanded range of types of futures have been created among a maelstrom of gambling contracts that have been developed from swaps, derivatives and other deals that sometimes facilitate real-world trade when they are used by manufacturing and commodity-moving firms as hedging devices; but which are mostly used simply for speculation by trader/gamblers, many of whom have been funded and loosely supervised by banks. This business made a great deal of money for thousands of the participants for a long run of years, especially between 1986 and 2008, and generated a great deal of taxation and consumer spending in the few centres of international business where it was encouraged.

This gambling was shown to be highly profitable, and it can make a significantly beneficial contribution to the economy: *but it must be properly taxed and controlled, as betting*. Until the market crash of 2006-8 financial conglomerates, especially in London and in the USA, mixed their betting with their stockbroking and corporate advisory business, and with banking. Both politicians and their disillusioned electorates have yet to understand that gambling business, however lucrative it may be, should be kept wholly separate from the balance sheets of both retail and investment banks. Banks and investment funds should be permitted to invest in specialist betting firms, as shareholders and possibly as bondholders; and should be eligible to place bets; but should not themselves be the bookmakers. An expanding range of 'wholesale' betting should be encouraged on the basis of a realistic set of rules, governed by strong, subtle regulators who are possessed of draconian powers. Properly managed gambling can be a huge source of international earnings for the London market, which has been the global leader in these innovations.

Keyns have no material substance: there may be certificates of their existence - such as charters and deeds that confirm land ownership or the status of a corporate entity, or paper share certificates and bank statement printouts - but the actual keyns are either *promises* or *declarations*. These are set out in contracts, and in assertions of ownership of ideas and of other intellectual property, and in other forms by which a legally enforceable right to own a keyn can be expressed. In an increasingly wide range of cases where records are electronically created and maintained, no paper instrument is required for the contract or the asserted ownership of financial assets or of intellectual property to be enforceable. The prices of new keyns - the terms that are agreed in completion of contracts - are based on the perceived security of the participants, weighted by the expectation of the parties as to how predictable economic events might affect their potential ability to maintain the status of the keyn over the proposed duration of the contract, and influenced by the present and anticipated levels of interest rates.

Within the parameters set by the law and by regulators, and heavily influenced by the incidence of taxation and the impact of monetary policy, people and corporate entities can create many forms of keyn [including gambling contracts] by sheer act of will. If I can find a firm or an individual that is willing to extend credit to me, I can create a debt. Every such contract creates a legally enforceable liability from me to the lender, which lasts throughout the life of the contract. A regulator may require my bank to give me a regular statement of the status of the loan that I have taken from the bank, with all the attendant liabilities that fall upon me, and to notify me of any change in terms - such as interest rates - that apply in accordance with the contract; but the primary responsibility for ensuring that the terms of the contract are met lies with me as its creator. Businesses and some categories of state agencies create keyns in the forms of shares, bills of exchange, letters of credit and a vast array of bonds, and other securities; which they sell to other economic entities and lease to their clients and to each other. Investment banking in the original meaning of the term is the management of these streams of financial business that facilitate investment and transactions in the material economy.

The market price of any existing keyn, on any day, depends on the potential buyer's current estimate of the capacity of the creator of the keyn to meet the terms of the contract under which the keyn was created: under current accounting conventions this is called the *fair value* of the keyn. Many financial contracts cannot have a 'fair value' in that sense: they depend on contingent events and are priced according to the perceived probability of the materialisation [or avoidance] of a particular outcome; and a huge proportion of the contracts are closed off or allowed to lapse long before they come to a point for settlement.

Virtually every personal or corporate estate carries debts: examples are a mortgage, or a credit card 'balance', or an overdraft; or repayment due to a bondholder, or obligations to employees, to shareholders or to other stakeholders; or an emergent debt to the taxman. Some keynic obligations are 'secured' by material assets: a house stands as security for the mortgage that is explicitly linked to the price for which it was bought; or a work of art may be designated as the security for a business loan. The debt is not owed by the asset, however, but by the person or organisation that created the debt; and the contract fails if the creator cannot ultimately settle it. Failures of this kind were the proximate cause of the crisis triggered by 'sub-prime' mortgage defaults by thousands of households in the USA in 2005-8. As that crisis developed, it became clear that banks had also made massive loans on commercial property [including hotel chains and department stores] where the 'valuation' of the asset was more extremely ridiculous than any house valuation that was to embarrass a retail mortgage lender.

Most payments from persons to financial institutions are instalments in a long-term process of repaying the principal and paying interest arising from the debtor's creation of liabilities in the past: the payments occur as direct debits and standing orders that absorb a significant proportion of the individual's available bank balance [or authorised access to credit] month by month. All keyns depend for their continuance in existence on the legal protection that is given to contractual rights, under the rule of law; and any economically active entity in a market economy can distinguish three sub-categories of keyn in its estate:

A] *ik: {an item of intellectual property, or intellectual capital}*; which is any legally enforceable status or right, including personal or corporate identity; and any concept, idea, image, process, design or literary work that can be defended at law as being the property of a person or an organisation of some kind. Patents, copyrights, trademarks and brands fall into this category.

B] *ka: keynic **assets***: assets that come into existence in accordance with the terms of a contract: these include bank deposits, shares, bonds, pension rights, entitlement to indemnification under insurance contracts and entitlements under gambling contracts, that can be recorded in the asset register of the estate.

C] *ko: keynic **obligations***: this category covers all the borrowings and debts that have been incurred by the estate, including the obligation to pay all consequential interest and service charges that are due when the time for each payment arrives. Commitments to meet gambling obligations, including historic obligations incurred in the course of 'casino banking', an all emergent obligations to pay taxes, are *ko*s.

[Note that *ik* is pronounced '*ick*' as in *quick*; *ka* as '*ca*' in *car*; and *ko* as '*co*' in *cocoa*.]

13

A debt is not normally forgiven in the event of the destruction or diminution of a specific asset that was put up as security when the **ko** was created. For example, the mortgage obligation that was incurred when one or more individuals bought a house remains outstanding even if recurrent flooding makes the house unsaleable, or a fire destroys it. All **ko**s that an estate owner has created become due for settlement when the estate is wound up; which occurs following the death of an individual human being, or the closure of a business or of a charity.

A regular verification of solvency is required to enable corporate businesses to retain the legal right to exist: each such entity must prove that it is a 'going concern'. Both corporations and individuals are normally required to submit evidence of solvency – being able to pay any bills that may fall due to be paid - before any other firm or person is willing to purchase a keyn that the would-be borrower wishes to create; and any buyer who fails to verify the security of the issuer deservedly bears a risk of default.

The net keyn position [**K**] of an economically active person or corporate body is derived from:

$$[ik + ka] - ko = K.$$

## 2. Jev

Pronounced like *'dev' in 'Devon'*.

In the middle of the nineteenth century, W S Jevons argued that the *value* of anything was the buyer's subjective assessment: "how much money is it worth *to me*, here and now?" Jevic valuation applies only to those classes of material assets for which the buyer's willingness-to-pay alone determines the price. The historic cost of production of the item is not relevant to jev pricing. The *jev* category includes a wide range of tangible things, new and old, that are variously categorised as:

- fine art [paintings, sculpture etc]
- antiques [including musical instruments, tools etc]
- archaeological finds
- geological, mineralogical and biological specimens
- memorabilia
- rare and special books
- incunabula
- manuscripts
- ephemera
- curios
- and other classes of 'collectibles'.

When any of these things is sold, it is priced exclusively by the amount of money that the keenest financially capable intending buyer is willing to pay for it. Buyers

14

are often guided towards the price they are willing to pay by the views of experts who verify the provenance and/or offer an opinion as to the 'quality' of the jev in relation to others in the same class; but the decision to make an offer for the jev is always taken by the buyer. For probate of a deceased person's estate, and for an insurance or tax valuation, each individual jev that is an inventoried item in an estate can be inferred to be worth approximately the same as the price that was agreed in the most recent sale of a closely similar object in the same category. The courts protect the ownership of jev-related *ik* [such as the right to claim copyright fees from sellers of reproductions of an artwork that the estate owns]; this is derived from the significant public and private wealth that is locked up in jev ownership. Acquiring jevs is part of the strategy by which wealthy individuals and some corporate entities accumulate and maintain broad portfolios of long-term assets. Legal costs may arise from verifying the provenance of works of art; or may be incurred in defining or defending the status of the artists and the authority of verifiers and valuers of their works.

Very many paintings, statues and other artworks by the greatest dead artists belong to museums and trusts that intend to own them permanently; hence relatively few such items come to market and when they do the price is usually determined by auction. Prices do not necessarily fall in subsequent auctions if a series of pieces by the same deceased artist happen to come on sale in the same year, because the price of each jev is determined exclusively by the competition between the potential buyers who bid for the particular item at the time of the sale. Successful living artists sometimes limit the amount of output that they produce, to keep the price per unit high; others, like Picasso, leave behind a huge stock of unsold pictures as an endowment for their children or for their favoured good causes, to be trickled onto the market at a rate that keeps prices high over many years.

Costs are incurred in maintaining many jevs. Delicate artefacts and works of art must be kept in controlled environments to minimise material degeneration, and many jevs have to be protected from thieves and vandals by active security measures. These costs are justified by owners because jevs retain their attractiveness to other buyers through time: a jev can be owned for many years; then sold to acquire cash with which the vendor can meet *ko* liabilities, or seize an emerging business or consumer opportunity. When a jev serves as security for a loan, the contract by which the keyn is created usually specifies that the jev must be insured; so that if the jev should be stolen or destroyed, the insurer makes available the cash that may then be required to settle the outstanding keynic obligation.

Some people have the majority of their estate in the form of jevs; and very many estates include some jevs: but the proportion of wealth that is represented by jevs in the asset register of a typical organisation or individual – compared to the valuation of keyns and quons in such estates – is usually small.

## 3. Quon

Pronounced with a short 'o' sound.: 'kwon'.

If a free person has access to a reasonably up-to-date phone and to an electricity supply that is sufficient to charge the batteries, plus an internet connection, that individual has access to all the knowledge that is in the net – almost everything that is known by the whole of humanity – and to a phenomenal range of entertainment, games, educational resources, culture, pornography and nonsense. The user may be in the most primitive shelter on a remote island, or in a billionaire's pad in Manhattan: both have access to abundant free data and to buy or to hire access to others' *ik* such as was never before accessible to even the most privileged members of their species. In the face of such access to intangible wealth, the once persuasive idea that economic science is concerned with the allocation of scarce material resources is redundant. Immaterial assets can be accessed and consumed in abundance, by anybody anywhere; subject to the limit of their spending power. Wherever *ik* is protected, it can yield revenue for its owners and for any franchisees or licensees; and that can be a target for taxation, and in many circumstances the assets are exposed to criminal extortion or to piracy [i.e. the breach of a patent or of copyright, or the unauthorised use of a trademark or brand].

A quon provides the consumer with:

1. the ownership, or a lease, of a physical asset that combines proprietary *ik* with the material components of the brand; or
2. the benefit [sometimes referred to as the *utility*] that is derived from being the recipient of a service function that deploys physical and/or mental activity by humans in combination with relevant proprietary *ik*; or
3. direct access by electronic means to immaterial *ik* such as downloaded music, games, videos and myriad 'aps'.

Consumers are conditioned to pay a significantly higher price for a prestigious quon than for an unbranded product that performs the same function. Suppliers of quons will only continue to provide their brand while the full cost of making units available is recovered from customers: including marketing and after-sales costs, and all the costs for defence and ongoing development of the brandowner's *ik*. This applies equally to immaterial quons that are accessed on the internet and to physical commodities. To consume quons is the aspiration of most individuals who know of the existence of branded lifestyle products and experiences. Even genuine ascetics, who have made a deliberate choice to eschew all forms of material consumerism, use the internet to communicate with like-minded fellows and to recruit disciples; and they control the dissemination of their ideas by maintaining copyright on their publications. Firms need to buy the patented and trademark-protected quonic machinery and supplies, and the copyright software that is needed to keep them competitive.

The desirability of *ephemeral* quons such as meals in a prestigious restaurant, pints of fashionably branded draught beer, and attendance to watch stars at concerts or sports events, is time-critical, time-limited and often specific to a location. The most *durable* quons – notably buildings, infrastructure assets and large items of capital equipment – can be maintained to hold that status for centuries; while many brands provide the specified consumer experience continuously over months or years, after which the material components and mechanical constituents may reasonably be expected to wear out: though many models become unfashionable before they are materially obsolete. Old tangible quons that have lost any second-hand marketability for their residual utility can become reclassified as jevs if they are kept in ownership until they become sufficiently scarce survivals that they gain the attribute of rarity; hence many people and some organisations selectively keep or collect what other people regard as junk in the hope that items will be transmogrified to jev status and become subject to that different pricing system. The *brand* by which a quon is identified may be the name of a designer, a restaurateur, a stage performer, a software designer, a pornographer or a company name; and often quons are recognised by a product name or *marque* [such as Ford's *Focus*] that was dreamed up for a specific model within the brand.

In service trades the material components of a quon are the equipment and materials deployed, for example, by a qualified provider of legal or medical services, who needs – at the very least – an office or clinical space, plus access to data sources and administrative facilities, and supplies; or by an entertainer such as a lap-dancer who performs in a protected environment.

Buying a quon that incorporates access to *ik* does not transfer the ownership of the *ik* as such: generally the *ik* remains the property of the brandowner, and of the patent holders and of any others who have created or purchased any of the intellectual capital. The quon buyer acquires ownership of an assembly of physical components or of services from human beings, through which it gains *access* to the *utility* - the consumer experience, or benefit - that is provided by the brand-protected *ik*.

Nothing but a recognised quon meets the full set of conditioned expectations of the sophisticated consumer, yet only a minority of consumers can afford to command a wholly quonic pattern of consumption that meets all their needs and aspirations. Most parents cannot routinely buy highly priced quons for everyday use by their children, so leading retailers offer their *own-brand products* that feature fashionable design, sturdy structure when that is appropriate, and a promise of replacement in the event of product failure. A store chain's self-certified foodstuffs and own-brand canned meats and electrical goods are **neoquons**. In the mature economies, specialist firms produce and package such products which they sell at marcomic prices [see the next category] to retail companies. The price of a neoquon is usually less than the price of a leading brand that offers similar functionality. Buyers of durable neoquons are often given the opportunity to purchase an extended warranty that will refund the price of the product, or replace the item, if it fails to deliver its specified performance during the cover period. This trading model is generally more profitable than is the establishment of brands that mimic [but do not exactly copy] prestigious quons, which are offered for sale at a lower price than the most fashionable brands. Some such second- and third-rank firms have achieved long term profit, when enough customers accept their more modest brand out of familiarity or as the best affordable option to which they can aspire: this trend is likely to increase as millions of consumers in the postindustrial societies get used to lower living standards, while governments encourage banks to fund start-up businesses that supply such brands. There is always a chance that a brand that begins this way might make the leap into a more-preferred market segment later.

## 4. Marcom

Marcoms are material commodities and manufactured products and services that are not protected from competition through being offered for sale in combination with significant *ik*, so they have none of the quonic utility to consumers that is conveyed by brands. This category of asset broadly covers what Marx called *commodities* and also applies to the *goods* and *widgets* of textbook Economics. This pricing category also includes 'seconds' and 'bankrupt stock' and out-of-time perishable items that were manufactured or prepared to be the material components of quons but did not make it through a point-of-sale as branded goods by a due date. The category also includes goods that are sold 'as seen' on market stalls and in discount stores. If capital were available to fund expanded production, the price of any 'good' in this category could be forced down by competition until price was equal to the exact cost incurred by the supplier who provides the last unit that can attract a buyer. In practice, producers would more probably stop expanding their capacity to produce before they reached the point where there was no surplus of income over costs and thus the market would never reach the spurious 'perfection' of an 'equilibrium price'. In a case where oversupply results from the progressive contraction of demand there might be a succession of coincidental prices at which supply exactly equals demand as factories close in succession; but none of these phases would be of any significant duration.

Billions of marcoms are incorporated into complex products every year, which will be sold as quons and neoquons. A whole chain of processes is performed to convert raw materials and detailed designs into the material components that ultimately form a sophisticated quon. Some firms are 'vertically integrated' so that the one organisation controls all the stages in a long sequence of production in their own plant; other firms outsource the supply of components, many of which they can buy 'just-in-time' from other firms. Sometimes an anticipated rise in demand fails to materialise, or is less than was planned for, and then the supplier's need for cash causes stock to be sold as 'surplus'. In some such cases a stock of fully assembled products may have been packed or labelled ready to be sold under a quonic brand before it is designated as surplus, after which it can only be sold at less than 'list price'. Supply chain management is important to most firms, and there are opportunities for firms to exploit suppliers and customers who lack vigilance and rigour.

All the way along the supply chain the expense of creating and storing, and sometimes of disposing of, surplus marcoms is accepted as a legitimate business cost because stock-piling is periodically necessary to ensure that a marcom-making firm, or a marcom-making division of a vertically integrated quon-providing firm, is able to meet surges in demand for the quon to which the marcom is a component. There is also a significant advantage to the supplier if some output can be stored during a short-term slump in demanded, to be used in response to a subsequent sales boom.

In the model world that features in so-called neoclassical free-market Economics a 'good' is put on sale in competition with virtually identical products from other makers, and only price differentiates the output from the different firms in the market; so all the producers come under pressure to drop their prices in order to obtain more sales. Iterative price cutting could in theory continue among producers until an 'equilibrium price' exactly covered the cost of providing the exact number of units that customers demand at that price. Even in theory such an equilibrium could only endure for seconds, until the next adjustment to the pattern of supply or of demand arises. Makers' marks are attached to some marcoms that are directly consumed and used by humans to enable the health, safety and other regulators to trace the goods back to their originators if something goes wrong. Increasingly precise regulation of retail sales and 'class actions' against manufacturers and distributors [often led by chancing lawyers] have caused many firms to cease to offer marcoms for direct human consumption due to the risk of being sued for causing detriment to a user. Retail chains address this risk by offering competitively priced *neoquons* under their own brands after checking them for health and safety compliance and for acceptability with customers. In cases where a category of marcom has been withdrawn completely from retail sale consumers must thereafter exist without that consumer experience. The withdrawal of consumer marcoms from the marketplace can have a significantly adverse effect on many humans' standards of living; especially for the poor.

As aggregate global output increases, a growing proportion of marcomic outputs serve as inputs to 'downstream' assemblies of quons; while [in general] a declining proportion of the increasing total output of marcoms is directly consumed by human beings as living standards rise. Quonmakers need to secure their supply chains, and thus it is in their interests to offer contracts on terms that enable their suppliers of inputs to maintain and renew their capital equipment, and treat their staff fairly. In the medium term demand for marcoms is constantly in flux due to the development of new input materials and new techniques, which lead to the obsolescence of manufacturing facilities. The introduction of new categories of quons and neoquons, and of new generations of established brands for which new or modified input components are required, also changes the demand for marcoms. Any marcom provider's market can also be affected by the entry of new competitors, and by changes in the pattern of demand for quons of which the marcoms are components, or by the introduction of new methods of marcom pro-duction, or the development of new input materials, or regulatory changes, or competitors' bankruptcies.

# CHAPTER TWO

# ECONOMIC INSTITUTIONS

### *The importance of the Law*

Civilisation has a greater need for the law than it does for democracy. People can live secure lives, with their property protected, as well under an absolute monarchy as under a constitutionally correct republic where the ruling power is a self-perpetuating oligarchy. While it is often claimed that a state where each registered adult has one vote, and the ruling Assembly is genuinely open to election by all adults, is the most likely to make laws that are seen by the people as being effective and fair, that is not a universal truth. Transparent and effective insurance laws, passed by Hitler's decree, served Germany well for over forty years and there are similar examples from past and present dictatorships all over the world. On the other hand, laws passed by a parliamentary majority that represents well under 50% of the electorate may be massively unpopular: as with Obamacare in the USA. Especially in areas relevant to business, the tsarist Russian method of creating a widely-based expert committee to formulate a law which is then imposed by decree can be optimally efficient; while lobbying of elected legislators by interested parties can produce seriously biased laws.

Below the level of legislation, much effective law is made as a result of court decisions and out-of-court settlements and arbitrations which are generally accepted as creating precedents that can be followed without litigation in future cases. Lawyers' inventiveness in creating work for their professions has been indispensable in developing the forms of contract that create and define keyns of all kinds. Personal identity exists because the law recognises persons. The concept that persons [including organisations] can create and own intellectual property - *ik* – is the highest economic achievement that has been made possible by the judicial system to date. The concepts that have become contemporary *ik* are derived from charters, licenses, patents and copyrights that were developed in early-modern Europe and subsequently taken to the colonised territories. These legal concoctions have made possible the emergence of an economy that is now dominated by quons and keyns; and the hope of permanent prosperity for all rests upon them. The validity of any *ka* or *ko* is entirely dependent on defensible contract terms; quons can only exist as symbiotic repositories of material possessions with integral access to *ik;* and neither jevs nor marcoms can be traded or insured properly if the legal ownership and status of such objects is uncertain.

These are crucial facts of productive economic activity that depend absolutely on the creativity of legal practitioners, in a world where the component of quon prices that is taken by the owner of the intellectual property that is embedded in the consumer experience often exceeds the total cost of the material components of the quon. Registering, regulating and defending intellectual property is crucial for businesses, and success in these actions makes some individuals very rich and some firms very profitable. Intellectual property is a vital component of personal, corporate and national capital; and the nation's wealth conspicuously includes the *ik* that is embedded in productive plant, and in the stimulation of productive new inventions. Further potential capital investment arises from the inflow of export earnings [and licence fees and remittances] that can be derived from the use of a country's intellectual property abroad.

## The Autonomy of Economic Agents

Economic agents are human individuals and legal persons [such as companies, government agencies, and societies] who are empowered to make decisions, own assets and enter into contracts within the economy. Demand for a vast range of both durable and ephemeral quons depends on the ability of potential customers to create debt to get the purchase price. Firms take on debts to acquire capital equipment and supplies; and individuals and households increase their consumption by creating debt. Such a process can be sustained whenever the increasing total of *kos* that are created by the firm or the individual is vindicated by the growth in their cash flow of income, backed up by increases in the perceived valuation of their assets, and for individuals the most conspicuous asset is residential property

In underdeveloped economies most human beings subsist on home-grown and homemade products; sometimes supplemented by purchases from a limited range of marcoms created by local craftsmen. The process of economic development from that traditional lifestyle to widespread branded quon consumption, that took centuries to come to completion in western Europe through the painful accumulation of circulating capital [accumulated by employers, partly at the expense of productive employees' living standards], can now be effected in emergent economies in a couple of decades. The fundamental shift in consumption patterns can be accelerated when it is financed principally by a massive expansion of lending to productive firms, and opening up consumers' access to mortgages, bank loans, hire purchase and credit cards. In the emergent countries there is a huge issue around the removal of people from the land that their families have tilled, or that their ancestors have roamed as hunter-gatherers, for many generations. Land is the primary necessity for urban development: but insensate land seizures during periods of rapid urbanisation create homeless families who lose their economic autonomy and form negative attitudes to the development process.

The majority of people in emergent countries eventually acquire assets and learn how to deploy them to gain access to credit that can expand their purchasing-power as consumers. Individuals who are targeted by advertising and promotion from social media can quickly pass to a phase in which lifestyle quons predominate; and immaterial solitary activities like on-line gambling or addiction to pornography can waste an individual's assets very quickly. Individual and corporate economic agents exist in space-and-time and are surrounded by risks, threats and opportunities. Differential access to education, information and means of communication influence the relative productiveness of human beings. The vast majority of producers of both intellectual and material outputs earn their livings as participants in firms. The primary contribution that a human individual who is managing his or her own assets, or a person acting as a principal or as a partner in a private business, or as the proprietor of a company, or as a corporate CEO, or as an hourly-paid operative, is to maximise the turnover that they can generate by deploying optimally the asset mix that their estate has inherited from the past period. The more fundamental objective, which was central to Political Economy before its usurpation by Economics, is to ensure that the productiveness of the estate's capital is being enhanced to improve the productiveness of its activities in the next period. While Economists and accountants focus on the cash turnover and the distributed or retained cash-accounted 'profit' that the business yields, Political Economy takes note of the extent to which the estate invests in genuine productive capability both in material terms and by enhancing the extent, the utility and the earning-power of its *ik*. The importance of this distinction will be apparent throughout this book.

Some individuals who have command of significant *ik*, which often comprises the ownership of their own name and image, are able to compete personally on a worldwide scale as leading sportsmen and women, popular film and stage artistes, successful authors, doctors with ground-breaking techniques and developers of social media or of computer games,: but they are some tens of thousands among seven billion souls. They depend on the community of states, as well as on their country of citizenship, to protect the *ik* that attaches to their names, their artistic creations, their copyrights and patents, and all their other assets. Those happy few can negotiate their own terms of employment, and their charges for granting access to their *ik*. For the rest of humanity, despite disparities of wealth between individuals, there is an essential dependency on the **wages fund** – the amount of the nation's output that can safely be allocated to the material consumption demands of the population *after allocating everything that is necessary to construct, maintain and repair materially and intellectually productive capital assets*, including the assets that will be needed to produce exports that will countervail the cost of imports. Economic policy in the United Kingdom since the Second World War has repeatedly stimulated short-term demand without due regard for the extent and the quality of concurrent investment. Thus imports have increased, especially in the many periods when credit creation has been accelerated, enabling importers to capture the market quickly while indigenous firms assess the extent and probable durability of the enhanced demand before they commit to investment. Sound policy would enable firms to allocate sufficient funds for timely investment; while ensuring that the wages fund [including the costs of national defence, law-and-order and the welfare state] is not more than the residual which remains after the necessary allocation to investment has been made. If consumption considerably exceeds the realistically-computed wages fund – as has probably occurred in every year in the UK between 1950 and the present day – the consequences of this reduction in the nation's capacity to generate wealth become apparent in the insufficiency of world-class new infrastructure, in the decay of industrial plant [with consequent loss of competitiveness by the firms that own them] and in the alienation of *ik* to foreign investors. An economy that has not invested sufficiently sucks in imports: which are paid for by state and personal borrowing, and by drawing-down savings including those that should be applied to securing future income through investment.

## Government, Governance and Regulation

The vast majority of individuals can only continue to make satisfying lifestyle choices by drawing upon a continuing allocation from the wages fund; and through most of history most people were allowed to draw from the fund only if they contributed effectively to the economy as producers, and/or as conservators of assets. Yet many millions of contemporary Europeans are under the impression that they live within a comprehensive welfare state, whereby if their personal resources are insufficient to provide them with the minimum standard of living that they expect, the state will ensure their comfort. A high level of comfort can only be provided for everyone if the national income includes a wages fund that is big enough to afford them that standard, year after year. If the combined economic activities of the whole population are not maintaining the necessary investment in future provision the time will surely come when either all of the population must take a cut in their living standard; or some groups of the population who are neither politically powerful nor economically productive must suffer disproportionate reductions in lifestyle. And meanwhile the politically powerful will be able to protect their position only by becoming more ruthless in their defence of their status, which requires them to remunerate those who support their power [including civil servants, lawyers, the police, the military and the taxation machine] from a top-slice of the wages fund.

The realities summarised in the preceding paragraph have emerged dramatically over the past six years, after having been obscured during the century in which Economics has been prevalent. Adam Smith is correctly described as the 'father of economics' because he is credited with having first proposed that the participants in economic life should be free to follow their perceived self-interest. He declared that this would ensure that the combined economic performance of an entire nation was optimised. This doctrine was quickly adopted 'in principle' by liberals as a maxim of good governance and around 1870 it mutated into the Economists' concept of 'rational' economic behaviour. But even before modern academic Economics was formulated the liberal dogma of free trade had been confronted by political and legal reality. Regulations and restrictions were found to be necessary to protect factory children from overwork and abuse, then night work for women was banned, then all workers were protected by laws which banned dangerous activities and the exposure of workers to toxic and abrasive substances. With the spread of democracy popular legislation that acted against free trade was consolidated by compulsory state education, by measures to promote public health, by compulsory unemployment insurance, by building regulations and by the enactment of thousands of other specific repudiations of untrammelled market freedom. The liberal political class failed to recognise the phenomenon that was the most fundamentally inimical to the concept of free trade: the rise of *ik*. The importance of intellectual capital – and of the means of defending it as the exclusive possession of its creators [and of those to whom the inventors sold or leased it] – became the most significant determiner of the wealth of individuals and the success or failure of thousands of firms. Economists simply piled up the accumulating heap of irrefutable evidence in the 'too difficult' tray and rolled out successively more arcane versions of their normative model.

The extent to which economic reality differs from Economics can be seen in the example of Charles Babbage [1791-1871] who is widely respected as the progenitor, rather than the direct inventor, of programmable computers. In popular accounts he was a very able individualist, who worked on his own for many years to design and build his 'engine'; until he had the good fortune to work with a brilliant woman who established much of the mathematical underpinning for future computer technology. But the British government was hugely interested in the project; not least because the French were also thought to be interested. Both countries thought that such devices would have immense military and civil potentialities if they could actually be brought into production. Babbage's research was subsidised by the government to the tune of £17,000: which a contemporary noted could have paid for a middle-scale warship. One would not suggest that the subsidy was equal to the billions we now spend on Type 45 destroyers, but it was a massive sum nevertheless. The extent to which invention and speculative research throughout the centuries has been funded by governments greatly exceeded the Research and Development budgets that were consciously set aside by companies until the middle of the twentieth century; and the paucity of both state funding and corporate investment for research now in the UK is another sure way of decelerating the growth of national wealth through the accretion of *ik.*

Accountants prepare balance sheets for businesses that include estimates of the resale prices that could be fetched by selling the assets and liabilities of the estate, expressed as a series of numbers of currency units. Most firms and tens of millions of individuals in the more mature economies were encouraged before 2007 to establish a net deficit on their estates' balance sheets; defying the common sense principle that households and firms should have a positive overall balance on the 'book value' of keyns plus quons plus marcoms plus jevs in their estate. If a person dies leaving more unsecured debt than the net valuation of his or her assets, their creditors have failed in the risk management of the credit that they extended to that individual. Before granting credit to any corporate or personal estate, the lender must verify the sufficiency of the assets that are held in the estate to serve as security for the new loan in addition to that assets that stand against all the borrower's existing debts, together with verifying the sufficiency and reliability of the borrower's anticipated income flow during the term of the loan; enabling him to service the loan in all likely circumstances.

Quons, jevs, and stocks of resalable marcoms, can serve as security for *kos* that a person or a firm creates; as can *ka*s that they own which were issued by third parties. The total valuation of quons [Q] and marcoms [M] and jevs [J] in an estate, plus-or-minus the net keyn position [K] of its owner, produces the **net balance [N]** for a person or for a corporate [or collective] entity:

$$\{Q + M + J\} +/- K = N$$

Companies must have a positive net balance at all times: trading when insolvent is illegal. State corporations and quangos usually have a governmental guarantee of solvency, backed up by supposedly rigorous control criteria. Any other form of organisation is viable if its overall **net valuation** is positive, according to conventional accounting standards; or in terms of this text if

$$\{ik + ka + Q + M + J\} - ko > 0$$

In the above:

K stands for **net** valuation of inventoried keyns: $K = \{ik+ka\} - ko$
Q stands for valuation of inventoried quons
M stands for valuation of inventoried marcoms
J stands for valuation of inventoried jevs.
*ik* is all forms of intellectual capital
*ko* is keynic liabilities
*ka* is keynic assets.

It is up to the potential lender, in any case, to verify that the valuation of a would-be borrower's assets is sound and truthful.

# CHAPTER THREE

# ECONOMIC DYNAMICS

The so-called classical Political Economists of the first three-quarters of the nineteenth century accepted as a basic fact of their existence the Law of Diminishing Returns; which the new-wave Economists thereafter also recognised, rather reluctantly, probably to be inherent in nature. The essence of this asserted law was that if over successive periods of time identical inputs of labour, capital and other resources were added to those that were required to increase production above the previous period's level, a point would be reached where the measured output attributable to the last standard set of incremental inputs would be less than for the previous set of additional inputs. Thereafter the increase in output attributable to each additional set of equal inputs would be less than from the previous set. It was assumed that if capitalists persisted in adding increments of inputs the successive returns would decline at an increasing rate. If they persisted nevertheless in adding inputs, a point would be reached where the net return to additional inputs was negative: the excessive use of plant, the crowding of human operatives, the increasing scarcity of supplies and other similar factors would mean that output actually declines as more inputs were piled in. This would clearly be a ludicrous situation, and realistically the Political Economists assumed that capitalists would switch the application of their resources to other activities at an early stage in the appearance of diminishing returns. Some writers also linked the phenomenon of diminishing returns to the universal operation in the physical universe of entropy; but it was not considered necessary to invoke that science to vindicate the Law of Diminishing Returns.

Even when the Law was taken as a 'given', however, Malthus and those of like mind argued that innovation in products and in the technology for providing products meant that it became worth investors' while putting their capital into the emergent industries and activities that deployed new *ik* rather than into an industry that was heading towards the point of diminishing returns. Hence over the economy as a whole there would be a momentum for progress that would provide increasing returns to well-directed investment in ever more sophisticated products and services and in technologically advanced methods. While many inventors did not have the knowledge or the resources to secure their intellectual properly in what they had invented, and thus gave their *ik* to humanity in general; increasingly it became the norm for *ik* to be acknowledged to its generators. In these circumstances, universities changed their staff contracts to give the institution a part [or even the whole] of the *ik* that was generated by their employees; and research councils and other funders also demanded to participate in the ownership of any intellectual property that was generated from the application of their funds. Similarly, as advanced research became concentrated in large firms' research units and in inter-firm research associations, the ownership of outcomes that could be secured as *ik* became a more significant issue.

In this century people far beyond the laggard 'Economics profession' are increasingly conscious of the negative returns that accrue to the social policies of the degenerate welfare state, and of the mounting tension between slowly-emergent and uncertain intellectual developments and the demand of a massively expanded human race to have not merely subsistence but a rising standard of living. That standard of living now includes more immaterial *ik* than could have been imagined even in 1990: the burgeoning of social media and on-line entertainment, which require just IT equipment [whose prices per byte are still declining] and electrical energy [whose supply is increasingly at risk due to the predations of taxmen and green campaigners]. It is noteworthy that Britain stands at a point where the future security of the electricity supply is in doubt: precisely because politicians have been terrified of making the necessary decisions in conditions of extreme economic uncertainty.

Paradoxically, while individuals and households in the richer countries increase their debts and save less, the economy at large is massively increasing the notional value of the immaterial instruments that are the stock-in-trade of the financial gambling industry. It has been notable that as the immaterial market has burgeoned, so the prices of properties have increased massively; such that they no longer reflect the cost of building the premises, but rather the availability of finance to enable a higher price to be paid for it.

Taking as a working hypothesis that while diminishing returns are generally avoided by a professionalised investment market, increasing returns can be gained by applying ever-advancing *ik* to both the material economy and the world of cyber-finance, this chapter seeks to explain in further detail to role and nature of immaterial assets in the contemporary world.

The keyn category of assets includes deeds of ownership of real estate, and certificates and computerised records confirming the ownership of all forms of *ik*; plus all financial instruments and 'products'; including currency notes, corporate and personal debts of all kinds including obligations incurred and assets gained in gambling deals. The scope and detail of sub-classes of keynic contracts is constantly changing, but the basic relationship of debtor and creditor, and the essential distinction between long-term and short-term contracts, does not change.

**A keynic asset** [*ka*] remains in existence for as long as the contract by which it was created remains in force:

- the creator of the *ka* accepts responsibility for the obligation or debt [*ko*] that they have accepted as the necessary concomitant to the advantage or asset that they have acquired by creating the *ka*; and

- the creditor to whom the contractual rights are assigned during the life of the contract owns the *ka*.

All through the period of existence of each *ka* interest and/or service charges and/or dividend payments and/or instalments of repayment and/or some other form of recompense - as specified under the terms of the contract - is due to the owner of the *ka* from its creator; or from another economically active entity that legally inherits or adopts the creator's obligation during the currency of the keyn. Many *ka*s expire on a specified date when the creator [or their successor] may be obliged to make a final settlement to the then owner of the asset.

Some keynic obligations arise not from contracts that are consciously entered into, but from lawful impositions that are placed on economic agents: such as a tax or license fee; or any legal liability that arises from the tenure of land or property, or in the course of parenthood or under a contract of employment, or from a variety of other situations. The obligation to pay a legally levied tax, fine or license fee falls due to be settled by a person or an institution. In a democratic state it is assumed that the taxpayer's consent to the imposition of levies, taxes and license fees has been expressed through the electoral process; and that each organisation is managed by people who accept their obligations to pay fees, fines and taxes as a necessary concomitant of their entity being recognised by the state as a legal person.

**Intellectual property** [*ik*] consists of the right of a human being or of a corporate entity to possess any of the following:

- the fundamental right of a human being to be a legal person: who then has the rights to own things and to make contracts;
- real property;
- the ownership of any product of intellectual activity [ by an individual or by employees acting on behalf of a firm] that is identifiable and definable, such as a copyright piece of writing, a design, or an advertising slogan; that the relevant courts can recognise and enforce as being exclusively the property of a human creator; or the property of an organisation to which the creators have contractually ceded control of their inventions and discoveries made within the context of their contract;
- ownership or control of any situation or status that is granted to the person or organisation under the law. Examples include patents and licenses to use patented processes, the license to practice as a doctor, extraction rights for oil or minerals or water, a franchise to run a branded coffee bar, or an employment contract;
- any other immaterial asset [not being *ka*] whose existence is recognised and defended by a properly empowered court.

- ***negative ik***: is an economic agent's liability in respect of any debt, including any unfulfilled component of a contract to provide cash or quons or
jevs or marcoms, or a contract to perform some service. If non-performance leads to a failure to fulfil the terms of a contract, the obligation can
potentially be transformed by a legal process into a debt, a ***ko*** that is given
a money 'valuation'.

Since all keyns are immaterial creations of human will, most of which are validated by legal formularies, they can have no intrinsic 'value'. The price at which any
keyn may be sold depends on the offer that a buyer is willing and competent to pay
in settlement at the time when the asset is put up for sale. Until about 1990, price
setting for any material or financial product was located at a point in the earth's
surface, and was thus fairly easily subjected to regulation by the regime on whose
territory the contract was made: but in cyberspace there is now a globally accessible marketplace, with many hundreds of millions of potential traders who have
widely differing levels of economic sophistication; and probably an even wider
range of ethical standpoints.

Market prices for keyns are stated in money; and monetary units are a sub-set
of keyns, in that they are immaterial promises issued by a government or a govern-
ment-licensed central bank. The number of currency units is usually stated on the
face of notes or on the dies that stamp coins but the usefulness of the money is
entirely dependent upon its credibility. That credibility, which can only be assessed
in terms of human beings' willingness to exchange any particular amount of any
country's money for goods or for another state's currency, or for a synthetic currency like bitcoin, depends on the ratio between the availability of goods in the
economy and the amount of money that the is accessible to the would-be buyers.

In daily life, even in the most sophisticated societies, despite the easy availability of non-cash means of payment for use by solvent firms and individuals, notes
and coins continue to circulate in massive volume. Cash is used by less sophisticated individuals who do not understand how to use electronic transactions. Much
more significantly, cash is king for drug dealers, secret gamblers, unauthorised
minicab drivers, ponces and their victims, recipients of disability benefit when they
do odd jobs, illegal immigrant workers, sellers of stolen goods and of fake watches,
and many other participants in the multi-billion pound black economy. The cash
that circulates from 'respectable' citizens into the black market slides back into
taxed areas of the economy through shops, street markets, pubs, bookies, box offices and other legitimate outlets that are still largely cash traders. The banks make
a charge for receiving cash from retailers, or for issuing change to them, because
handling cash is time consuming; cash also brings a risk of robbery, occupies physical space and is dirty. Yet notwithstanding their efforts to reduce the extent to
which their customers require them to trade in notes and coins, the retail banks
provide access to cash for small business's tills and for personal customers who insist on having ready money to buy drinks in the pub and vegetables on the market;
and also to pay for drugs and commercial sex and for untaxed cleaning or plumbing

services in a way that avoids their spending pattern being tracked through the record of their debit and credit card transactions. Bank notes are also used for inhaling white powder.

Despite the survival of physical cash, the majority of significant legitimate purchases within a mature market economy are settled by making transfers of bank balances: payment by mobile phone, debit card, BACS transfer, credit card, cheque, banker's draft, direct debit, standing order and other means that are authenticated signals to banks to make transfers of balances from one named and numbered account to another. From this arises banks' power to create credit, which operates as pseudo-money for as long as the credibility of the system is maintained. Bankers are expected to abide by rules and guidelines set by their government or their central bank or by a subsidiary regulator. If they operate strictly within the rules they rely on the state or the central bank to guarantee the credit that they have created. Historically, banks encouraged long-term depositors to hold accounts which yielded a higher rate of interest but required notice of withdrawal, giving the bank a better chance to match inward and outward flows of liquidity. But from the nineteen-seventies, and culminating in the first years of the present millennium, there was a perception that clever bankers had ended the need to accumulate savings from the mass of the population and from firms. They now had the process of *securitisation* by which retail banks could sell their ownership of their customers' negative balances into the wholesale market; and consequently retail banking customers were offered such easy access to credit that millions of them saw no point in saving-up to buy desired assets for cash.

Contract law requires that there are two parties to any transaction: a buyer who is to receive some service or asset or other perceived benefit; and a seller who is to deliver the service or the asset to the buyer. The seller is required to *perform* whatever it is that they promise under the contract, for which the buyer is obliged to pay the *consideration* that is the agreed price for the performance. There might be a significant period of time between making a contract and the date when the final delivery of performance is due, which is usually the date and time when the final component of the consideration is due to be paid. A contract to supply a new fleet of aircraft or to build a major bridge takes several years to complete, and modern contract terms are structured to enable the two parties to complete the deal even though both the job specification for the project and the purchasing power of money may change dramatically during the contract period. Both parties to long-running supply contracts are aware that economic and political conditions may change significantly during the contract period. The buyer wants to be as sure as possible that he can make payments in the specified currency on the due dates while managing the risks that regulatory change, or inflation, or deflation or currency fluctuations will make future settlements more expensive than had been anticipated at the time the contract was negotiated. The supplier wants to reduce the risk of having to pay higher than estimated future prices for input materials and for labour, and to be able to make up for delays due to unusually adverse weather or to political problems – possibly including terrorism – by managing purchases to take account of deviations from the critical path that is planned for the project. Hence the treasurers and finance directors of large non-financial organisations use sophisticated keyns, including some gambling deals, to mitigate the perceived risk of potential variances in future prices and input costs that could derail their tightly budgeted business plans.

In the nineteen-seventies some adventurous traders devised *derivatives* to facilitate speculative bets that were each *derived* from a data-set following the movement of prices for a real-world contract type. Subsequent phases of development added more speculative risks, extending into exchanges and events of a purely financial nature. Derivatives are akin to *spread bets* that also enable punters [many of whom are traders employed and funded by firms in the securities industry] to speculate on movements in financial markets and in commodity prices. Clever programmers create algorithms that enable machines to trade currencies and novelty financial products with each other at vastly higher speeds than human brains could encompass: which require the creation of even more sophisticated programs supposedly to prevent such high-speed trading from running wild and undermining the system. The vast majority of the contracts that are traded have no role in funding industrial investment or the construction industry, or even the welfare state.

In the late 1990s traders began to issue what grew to become many billions of dollarsworth of 'products' created by *structured investment vehicles* [**SIVs**]. Each SIV acquired a separate legal identity when it was created initially for specific purposes, such as wholesale funding for 'bundles' of securitised mortgages and credit card debts. The transfer of bank balances that retail firms [banks and building societies] received from the sale of their customers' debts enabled the lenders to issue more loans, which meant that they acquired more **ka**s created by individuals and by small to medium-sized firms that could subsequently be bundled together in further securitisations. An increasing proportion of the securities that were created in this way were resold – often several times over - to become consolidated into **CDOs** [*collateralised debt obligations*] and **CLOs** [*collateralised loan obligations*] issued by SIVs and by *funds of funds*, most of which were affiliates or spin-offs of securities firms and of hedge funds.

Programs were adopted by all the major banks and securities traders that supposedly rationalised their attempts to achieve a rolling match of maturities of assets against liabilities across all their terrestrial and cyberworld contracts. The balance of **ka** with **ko** was verified by a real-time assessment of **VaR:** the perceived total '*value-at-risk*'. **VaR** provided a summary estimate of the supposed 'fair valuation' of an organisation's portfolio of assets and of contingent liabilities, derived from the current market prices that all the assets would fetch and the maximum possible loss that the organisation would face if it had to pay out on all the bets that it had underwritten. This assessment was supported by forecasts of whether the **ka**s and the **ko**s in the firm's book of business would continue to balance at a series of time points in the future if no further contracts were entered into and assuming that the regulatory and macroeconomic context remained stable. This indicated which sorts of transaction should be added to the existing portfolio to eradicate adverse potential future imbalances arising from the contracts that had been made. By 2005 the methodology had been extended in some banks and securities firms to postulate a **TCE**, a *tail condition expectation*, or **Tail VaR**; which alongside other complex methods of risk evaluation compelled them to recognise - when the 'crunch' struck - how seriously they had mismanaged their portfolios.

In the period before the crisis of 2006-8 the financial conglomerates received profits from retail banking and from selling their advisory services. The accumulation of profits from those activities enabled their retail affiliates and associates to make increasingly reckless loans for home-buyers and in the field of commercial property. They enthusiastically engaged in securitisations of retail bank debts and pushed new bond and share issues from non-financial businesses into the collective savers' market. Then they churned the business again by repacking all these categories of 'product' into new asset classes for onward sale. While there was modest expansion of the total stock of housing, most of the massive increase in the perceived 'value' of the housing stock was simply produced by inflating property prices. The permitted modest expansion of the officially recorded money supply was greatly magnified by the ways in which the financial markets could increase the velocity of circulation of money. The wholesale financial market offered securitisation to retail lenders, some of whom offered 110% mortgages to individuals who self-certified their earnings. A torrent of propaganda assured owner-occupiers who did not move home that their *equity* in their homes was increasing in step with the rise in prices of the similar properties that were sold. Home owners were encouraged to exploit their 'equity' [the amount by which the 'valuation' of their house exceeded their mortgage debt] by using their credit cards to buy and to hire more quons.

Traditional wisdom, based on frequently-painful experience, requires the regulating monetary authority in every country [or monetary union] to correct or to close a bank that fails to maintain the required *reserve ratio*. Every bank must have unrestricted access to greater notional 'value' in **kas** than it owes in **kos,** counting shareholders' capital for this purpose as **ko**; and of that total of assets they must have a set percentage in immediately accessible purchasing power – the reserve ratio. The old rules and ratios were increasingly sidestepped and avoided as the expansion of credit became more frenetic down through 2007; while regulators either failed to see breaches of the rules, or turned a blind eye to them. It became apparent in September 2008 that the majority of large banks in Europe and the USA had exposed themselves to incalculable liabilities. Some of them had indulged in incompetent lending to borrowers who had insufficient capital, and all of them had extended the range and riskiness of loans that they made to speculative borrowers. In absolute contravention of centuries of experience and of common sense, firms that were registered and regulated as banks had *borrowed short* and *lent long*.

They had borrowed [largely from each other] to buy assets, including bundles of securitised mortgages, which were suddenly recognised to be illiquid. They had also used some of their easily-acquired lending capacity to finance corporate take-overs, and to fund many sharp practices in their traditional banking markets. Cunning devices were developed shortly before the crash, supposedly to 'insure' some of these contracts in the event of default. One of the most conspicuous of these, *credit default swaps* were untested; and in the event they proved to be more fallibly speculative than most other new contract types: they failed, threatening the USA with a total systemic collapse of the financial system: hence the federal authorities had to intervene.

In the midst of the chaos that was consequent on the market crash, however, a phenomenon of global significance emerged from the shadows. The banks and fi-nancial corporations had created trillions of dollarsworth of **'off-balance-sheet products'** – bets - [derivatives etc] that followed the paradigms of market behav-iour rather than the prices of real-world assets; and these were in many cases unaffected by the crash. The traders who had created and dealt in these instru-ments had been paid large commissions in recognition of the turnover that they recorded. Because these commissions were often miscalled bonuses, envy com-bined with incomprehension as politicians, the press and the general public united in 2010–2014 to revile the 'bankers' who continued to trade [albeit more cau-tiously] in these products, and to be massively rewarded for doing so. The profits that continued to be accrued from that business were the main internal source from which the reorganised banks could rebuild their reserves to the higher levels that were set in the revised Basle standards: but 'casino banking' was widely tra-duced as an incomprehensible and evil trade that should be suppressed. Given the revulsion of the ignorant herd of critics, it is unsurprising that the practitioners in the global betting business have not been keen too publicly or too stridently to de-fend their activities. But for the future economic health of Britain it is imperative that the key facts do gain acceptance, and that policies are adopted that will enable the London-based international market to grow as a major source of earnings that can help to rebuild the nation's capital resources. The British government has re-peatedly vowed to 'protect' the City of London from unduly restrictive, often envious, EU regulations and taxes. But the apparently inexorable rise of the un-comprehending Brussels federalisers has put the City's trades in serious danger. Some of the UK politicians who should be opposing them have not had the wit or the courage frankly to identify, protect and promote derivatives and other specu-lative 'investments' for what they are.

The relationship of money to other assets is governed by Fisher's Law: [aka the *Quantity Theory of Money*]. The Law is summarised in the simple equation:

$$MV = PT$$

Where M is money supply, V is velocity of circulation [of all media that can be deployed as money], P is the level of prices, and T is the number of transactions at those prices. None of these quanta is constant, they are constantly changing and no exact measure can be stated. But, as with barometric pressure, an expert observer can see whether it is rising or falling and by approximately how much, and whether the rate of increase or diminution is accelerating or declining. Between 1976 and 2008, while central bankers purported to control the media of exchange that fell within their definitions of **M**, they effectively ignored **V**. The regulators' incomprehension of the essential facts about the system left the commercial banks and other lenders free to churn the balances that they made available to each other ever more speedily, while keeping the notional total of officially-recorded **M** within the stated target range. Some of the incremental turnover was used by the wholesale financial market to securitise loans and mortgages that were issued to the public by retail banks [and by building societies, savings and loan companies, and similar businesses], and by credit card companies and by a huge raft of other licensed lenders; all of which became increasingly adventurous in the types of contract that they created with firms and with individuals.

Between the nineteen-seventies and the crash of 2006-8 various lobbies and interests produced dozens of definitions of *'the money supply'* – **M** - ranging from:

- banknotes and coins only,
- widening to banknotes plus coins plus bank deposits,
- extending to ever- wider definitions that included all types of 'instruments' that may be traded by banks and securities brokers; including more betting contracts.

The *velocity of circulation* [**V**] had been relatively simple to estimate, and was generally an accurate indicator, when **M** [the historically-defined money supply] had been constrained by the availability of gold which was key to the gold standard system. But **V** was increasingly ignored after the final abandonment of the gold standard in 1971, especially after the 'big bang' in 1986. Most of the people who worked in the securities industry and in banks, and in central banks and in regulatory bodies, did not realise that most of the expansion of turnover and most of the growth of 'asset value' and of 'value-at-risk' in the financial services sector derived from accelerated **V**.

Under Fisher's Law, if an increase in the supply of money [**M**] and/or in the velocity of circulation of a growing variety of means of making payments [**V**] is significantly greater [or less] than the rate of growth in the supply of goods and services in the economy, the resulting imbalance **must** impact on prices [**P**] and/or on the amount of trade [**T**] that takes place. Price stability can only be maintained if the effective money supply that is accessible to economic agents in any period - **M** multiplied by **V** - increases [or diminishes] in line with the growth [or the decline] of activity [**T**] in which human beings and firms participate. Whichever definition of **M** is selected for any expository or regulatory purpose, if the product of **M** times **V** increases more than the increase in **T**, the prices at which transactions can be concluded [**P**] must go up. If **M** expands faster than **T**, price inflation can only be avoided if **V** decelerates at the rate that compensates for the potential impact of the excess of **M**. The great delusion that enabled the millenarian debt bubble to become so destructive was that 'monetarist' regulators felt so cocksure about their mastery of their naively-defined '*money supply*' that they effectively ignored the constantly-varying [usually increasing] rate at which power-to-borrow was developing; yet it was precisely the market's expansion of the range of types of immaterial transaction that facilitated and accelerated **V** to the extent that made the 2007 crisis inevitable.

During the slump in the nineteen thirties, as unemployment increased the aggregate purchasing power of the population declined. The velocity of circulation and the number of transactions declined as firms and individuals ceased borrowing [and would probably have been refused, if they had asked for loans], and as firms had to compete harder for sales there was downward pressure on prices. Central bankers were determined to prevent hyperinflation, a situation where the available money supply significantly exceeds the demand of the economy to hold cash causing prices rapidly to increase to absorb the excess of cash. When the global economy went into recession, central bankers were reduced the money supply in line with the shrinkage of the economy; which further intensified the depression. As **P** and **T** were declining, a deceleration in **V** was inevitable as millions of people reduced the number of transactions as their incomes and expectations declined. In these conditions Keynes proposed that the key to economic recovery would be psychological; depressed people must be stimulated into optimistic behaviour. Both in their personal spending and in releasing funds from the firms that they control, market participants are likely to spend more of the available money sooner if they expect their own incomes and the trade that they do to increase thereafter. Keynes' *General Theory of Employment, Interest and Money* postulated that a judicious combination of increased M [released into the system by carefully planned government spending] and active management of interest rates could support the necessary acceleration of **V** by unlocking unused circulating capital to pay for wages and commodities that would cause further demand to appear in the economy through the *multiplier* effect. The authorities should also be willing to increase **M** as much as may prove necessary, once the economy was expanding again, to prevent **P** from rising disruptively. The accelerator for speeding **V** could be applied judiciously to encourage the economy to grow until it came close to *full-employment equilibrium*: at which point the brakes [reduced state spending and higher interest rates and tighter control of the money supply and increased taxation] should be applied in order to prevent *overheating*.

The 'thirties slump was widely regarded as the immediate cause of the unemployment that brought the Nazi Party to power in Germany, thus causing the Second World War which caused so much death and destruction of wealth. After the war governments were anxious to ensure that economic growth was restored. The crass implementation of that policy in the UK was designed to buy votes for the politicians who were in power by enabling the electorate to increase their consumption of quons at a rate that exceeded the capacity of domestic industry to supply them. This process was intensified as more of the national income was allocated to consumption, so progressively over time there was less capital available for producing better-designed and more-advanced domestically-produced quons that could be marketed quickly to match the increase in consumers' spending-power. This opened the way for competitive imports to make greater inroads into the UK and increased the shift to the consumption of imports and away from investment.

In Germany the greater material and human devastation that accompanied total defeat in 1945 made the electorate more willing to accept an emphatic concentration on investment - especially in heavy capital industries in the first instance - that so miraculously restored the fortunes of the Federal Republic by 1980. Other democratic European countries adopted policies in a spectrum between the German and the British examples which led to differential success as manifested by their firms' capacity to ride out, or be sunk by, the crisis of 2006-8. As the turnover in their economies had increased before 2006 governments expected their central banks constantly to permit an increasing monetary circulation. In Germany this was largely directed through regional banks that were expected to ensure a concentration of investment in industry, while British financial firms were progressively enabled to increase available spending-power by introducing new products that increased the velocity of circulation and thus enabled a more rapid increase in consumers' transactions to take place. Extraordinary credence was given to *credit rating agencies*, especially in the USA and the UK; these for-profit firms purported independently to assess the strength of other firms and of financial assets. Early this century most of them abjectly failed to recognise emergent disasters in *Independent Insurance* in the UK, and globally in US-based *Enron*. Blithely they continued to offer good ratings to insubstantial 'securities' and to their issuers. The massive global insurance corporation, *AIG*, was highly rated until the week of its collapse, disregarding the fact that a small peripheral division of the firm had underwritten a vast amount of bankers' debt through selling a new class of betting slips [credit default swaps] which wiped out the group's massive balance sheet. When that calamity occurred the US government decided that the disruption caused by a failure of *AIG* would be so damaging to the economy that the group was rescued, at an initial cost of hundreds of billions of dollars. Subsequently the agencies pretended that they had never meant their ratings to be interpreted as authoritatively as they had been, thus confirming that there is no valid independent method for assessing the relative security [or the potential future prices] of *kas*. Before the crisis it was reckless and deeply shameful that government-appointed regulators in the most sophisticated financial markets treated the ratings as authoritative; and it is inexcusable that any regulator should continue to do so now. But they do, because there is nothing else to maintain the concept of 'value' in what Economists proclaim to be 'rational' markets.

Keynes referred to 'irrational optimism' as a major factor in creating booms in asset prices. Developing that point in the next generation, Hyman Minsky spent a long academic career beginning in the nineteen-fifties examining these crucial relationships, largely ignored by the mainstream of the 'Economics profession'. Ten years after his death, in the wake of the 2006-8 crisis, his work began adequately to be recognised; with an increasing number of Economists admitting that there had been a 'Minsky Moment' as the inevitable consequence of the failure by market regulators and by participants in markets to understand the relationship between keynic assets, debt, time and money. As Minsky had foretold, during the boom of 2002-8 financial institutions massively increased both the volume and the variety of the keyns that they created and the range of purposes for which they would advance loans. The available money supply could only stretch to meet the demand of the finance sector for liquidity [given that 'monetarist' controls on **M** remained in force in the UK and the US where the new markets were the most vigorous] so long as exuberance among traders and bankers permitted unprecedented increases in **V**. Assuming that participants in a booming market borrow to enable them to participate in the accumulation of assets, Minsky classified borrowers in three broad groups:

1.  "Hedge borrowers": firms and individuals who can pay the interest, and if necessary repay the principal of their loan in cash derived from their asset portfolios;
2.  "Speculative borrowers" whose incomes normally enable them to service the debt, but who need to re-borrow or roll-forward their loans because the balance-sheet of their firm or estate is not sufficient to enable them to close off the loan at their discretion. People and firms get themselves into this situation when they assume that in the medium term the asset that was bought with the borrowed sum will appreciate in price sufficiently to enable them to settle the debt when they sell the asset [and, if they have planned well and been lucky, make a profit for themselves as well];
3.  "Ponzi borrowers" who rely on the resale price of the asset rising sufficiently to enable them to service the debt [both interest and capital repayment].

Minsky showed how, when an asset bubble collapses and prices begin to fall, the most extreme Ponzi borrowers are immediately unable to service their debts: they also find that they are unable to pass on their day-to-day liabilities through engaging in in more trading. Then it becomes clear that they do not have the means of meeting the demands for cash to which they have been committed by contracts. As the Ponzi firms fail the viability of speculative borrowers next comes under challenge: and some of them become unable to service their debts because the prices of the assets that they do own continue to fall; so the cash that they can get in the market from liquidating assets is insufficient to meet their need. Finally if market prices for the most secure financial products fall far enough some previously-covered borrowers could also be unable to meet their obligations. The collapse of confidence and of prices could become total.

Minsky pointed out that during a boom houses are treated as speculative assets whose prices rise in proportion to the increase in the amount that financial institutions lend to property purchasers. In those conditions house prices have no equivalence with the material cost of constructing the houses. Especially in the period 2001-6 lenders increased the 'valuation' of property assets, including hotels, shops and industrial units, as they lent more on looser terms to wider categories of borrowers. The boom in the USA and in parts of Europe that peaked in 2005-6 was greater than any previous bubble largely because securitisation enabled primary lenders to transfer the debt on the loans to the other market participants who bought the securities. Mortgagees' debt and credit-card debt became progressively more widely spread around the wholesale market: so more and more firms became at risk when the expansionary mood gave way to pessimism. When the mood-shift happened [triggered by defaults on sub-prime mortgages in the USA] the prices of the weakest financial products collapsed; and the fact that all property assets were perceived to be potentially 'over-valued' meant that the collapse of 'value' spread virally. Neither regulators nor the majority of risk managers in financial firms anticipated the bubble ending as it did, in a Minsky Moment; and consequently those firms reaped the whirlwind. Governments allowed a few significant corporations to collapse, but very quickly they recognised that economic stability as such was at risk. Consequently they shored surviving firms up with loans, or by facilitating mergers with banks; and in some cases by partial nationalisation of 'rationalised' corporations. In the same period the International Monetary Fund and the European Union [acting together with the European Central Bank in eurozone countries] forced the countries where the credit-creation system was most over-extended compared to their actual resources to restructure their sovereign debt. Such restructuring worked to the relative disadvantage of domestic bond-owners, including pension funds and trade union reserves, whose assets declined massively in price and in future income-generating potential. Cynical speculators, most conspicuously alien hedge funds, bought 'distressed' government bonds at knock-down prices; then they stated their terms for selling the bonds back the issuer governments. They were seeking a profit and had no interest in making it easy for the governments to restructure and rationalise their debts on terms that would be easier to meet. This led to a series of stand-offs, some of which continue as this text is written.

The most-stressed European countries in 2009 - Ireland, Spain, Portugal, Greece and Cyprus – had joined the eurozone on its initiation, so they had no control over the amount of the currency that was in circulation and in which personal, corporate and government debt in their own countries was denominated. They could not devalue their currencies, which was the historically well-proven way of reducing the cost of debt owed to aliens; nor could they adopt trade restrictions that defied the rules of the EU. Thus they had to submit to German-led demands for austerity, from which the adverse social and political consequences will be long-lasting. Again commentators and citizens demanded that there should be a more rational system that did not allow 'irresponsible, grasping bankers' to lead whole countries to catastrophe. Even in the latest crisis of the global financial system there has been no hint of a will on the part of politicians to surrender control of their national or community currencies to an International Reserve Bank. The euro is the exact reverse of a step towards a global currency: it was created before the boom reached its peak and it is a vital component in the structure of the *Festung Europa* that has been built to limit the exposure of the EU to the competitive tempest that will batter most of the postindustrial countries over the coming decades. The creation of the eurozone was a political project and the adoption of the euro was accompanied by so much false presentation of data by applicant governments and by some central banks, that the failure of casino banking in 2007 inevitably exposed the flakiness of the common currency. It disclosed some of the lies on which the eurozone was constructed; and the legacy from that history of unsustainable falsehood may yet bring about the collapse of the system.

The **solvency** of any estate – or any country - can in principle be estimated when a guesstimate is made of the market price that could be fetched for the total of intellectual property [*ik*] that is owned by the business or by the people and firms domiciled in the country, plus its financial assets [*ka*] and the current estimate of the potential resale price of its holdings of quons and jevs and marcoms: and the entity is solvent if the aggregate of those things exceeds the aggregate *ko*:

$$[ko - [ka+ik+Q+J+M] ) > o$$

A person can only legally acquire the liquidity with which to make an increment to their pattern of consumption; or to meet an unexpected and unavoidable obligation to pay a debt, fine or tax, by adopting one or more of the following means:

- sell material assets, usually quons or jevs: with the opportunity-cost of having ready cash but no longer having those assets;
- sell *ka*s, such as bank deposits, bonds or shares: the opportunity-cost of this option is surrendering any maturity premium that might accrue to owners at the point when they *ka* is liquidated;
- take out a mortgage or loan or hire purchase agreement: the opportunity-cost is that future income will be committed to servicing this *ko* throughout the contract period;
- hire the quon: which commits a slice of future income throughout the contract period and might provide less complete control over the consumer experience than does outright ownership;
- increase earned income: by expending greater effort, and/or spending more time at work: with the opportunity-cost of allocating less time and probably less energy for lifestyle activities.

Most of these options became inaccessible to many individuals and businesses in the Atlantic economies after 2007. While the decline in City employment in the UK was exploited by independent school headmasters to recruit a few numerate schoolteachers, many more people saw little benefit in acquiring career-orientated qualifications that were already heavily oversupplied; and it became hard for the unemployed to gain valid work-related experience.

The decline in saving among the mass of citizens is one of the most significant changes that took place in the twentieth century. In 1914, 40% of British households had at least one *Prudential* saving or insurance product, and at least another 30% of households were covered by other home-service assurance companies. By the millennium *Prudential's* penetration had declined to 14% of households [many of these holding only old policies on which collection cost exceeded the premium received]; and the overall coverage of households by life assurance was declining as policies lapsed, matured, terminated, or were paid out on the death of the assured individual. Savings and investments by households decreased from the later nineteen fifties. The 'stakeholder' savings and pensions plans that were devised for lower earners under the aegis of the Blair government made no significant contribution to the replacement of the abandoned savings culture among the population. Ditto can be expected from the attempts of the 2010 coalition to force the low-paid to contribute to petty pension pots. The most conspicuous [but quantitatively trivial] take-up of stakeholder plans has been as a tax-beneficial avenue for modest intergenerational cash transfer from grandparents to their descendants in an affluent minority.

Millions of people who saved voluntarily, through their pension funds and in other ways before 2008, saw that their funds' investments had greatly been diminished after the crunch; and many thousands among them are sufficiently sophisticated to recognise that a worse personal impact of the financial collapse will probably be experienced when significant inflation [potentially hyperinflation] circumvents obligations to savers at some date in the future. All this will make it more difficult for the economy to achieve sustainable long-term growth. Textbook Economics offers no help with this conundrum: but fortunately many thousands of women and men who are known as 'economists' have developed practical skills and useful knowledge, and could apply their skill and experience to assist in the formulation of viable policies that can mitigate the potential crisis; if they finally free themselves from the Smith-Marshall dogma that has blighted the economy for the past century.

# CHAPTER FOUR

# BRANDS IN THEIR CONTEXT

The increasing cohort of consumers who have chosen 'organic' milk and vegetables, and 'fair trade' coffee, require certification that their purchases meet these preferences: certificates of verification of origin for such products make them a class of *ik*; so buyers who make these options have voluntarily extended the scope of product certification of which branding is a part. No material thing that is consumed by humans in the modern urban economy is a simple 'gift of nature' that is gathered and used without the intermediation of other people and of corporations; or without the use of capital equipment, and free from licensing systems and legal authority. 'Fresh air' is available only because governments enforce costly pollution control. If I grow lettuce in my garden – which is mine according to land law, and has planning consent for horticulture - I may use only genetically approved seed. My use of water from my own well or water butt is controlled under abstraction regulations and health and safety laws, and any fertilisers that I use must conform to licensed standards. Even if one could ignore taxation and interventionist state spending, regulative restrictions would still be pervasive; even in domestic life, in a free country.

Water and minerals are available on and under the land and beneath the oceans thanks to the 'bounty of nature', but their extraction depends upon a complex of keynic, quonic and marcomic transactions. By the time a consignment of iron ore has been extracted from Australia and put on a train for shipment to Korea, the process has incurred [at least] the following costs:

- *ik* purchases and exposures
    - fees for exploration licenses;
    - fees for verification of the legal status of the land;
    - fees for confirmation of the landowner's right to extract the material;
    - royalties to the landowner;
    - regulatory fees and payments;
    - tax;
    - compulsory insurance premiums;

- o   licenses [company registration, planning consents, extraction licence];
- o   payments to any trade association or cartel;
- o   {and, in many countries, bribes}
- prices paid for
  - o   quon purchases
  - o   specialist exploration services;
  - o   branded equipment;
  - o   engineering consultancy and services;
  - o   skilled management and labour;
  - o   unskilled labour;
  - o   risk management services;
  - o   optional insurance premiums    [and any alternative risk financing];
  - o   transport services;
  - o   energy supply;
  - o   water [and/or water abstraction rights, which are *ik*].

keynic exposures where the activity can only occur when it is funded from either shareholders' resources or from borrowed capital;

marcom purchases: payments for items used in mining, processing and transportation that do not incorporate quonic *ik* and are therefore used at the extracting firm's risk.

Academic Economists build their 'analysis' of the functioning of imaginary business entities by assuming that the sole purpose of the producers of goods and services is to present their output at the point-of-sale where autonomous buyers review competing supplies and engage in transactions on the basis of two unrealistic assumptions:

- that the participants in a transaction have access to all the information that could conceivably influence their decision;
- that in a 'unit of time' each decision-taker [a buyer or a seller] concentrates solely on the potential costs and benefits of entering into this transaction, and is under no external pressure [such as hunger, exhaustion, thirst, sexual stimulation, taxation or coercion].

Models built on this base have been expanded into millions of words and set out in highly complex criteria for competitiveness: on which basis recent generations of Economists have asserted that 'imperfect' reality should so be regulated that actual market behaviour would be compelled to approximate to the model: that is nonsense and the 'efficient markets hypothesis' now has more detractors that advocates.

Human beings have animal needs; and they are affected by competitive and collaborative instincts, imperfect knowledge, differential education and intellectual competence; and they are constantly consciousness of the myriad options, opportunities and pressures that they experience simultaneously. Both on their own account and as managers of corporate entities, human individuals make pragmatic decisions; with a varying awareness of [and appetite for] risk in different contexts and at different phases in their life cycles and their careers.

Right from the first stages of designing a consumer product or experience that is to be offered for purchase as a quon, precautions are built-in to minimise the risk that consumers will claim redress for detriment arising from their use of [or exposure to] the brand. Hence with notable exceptions - such as tobacco products and high-risk sports - marketing campaigns usually stress the safety and reliability of quons. Educating consumers in the safe use of the product is often an important part of the marketing and after-sales process. Customer complaints are dealt with promptly, warranties are acted upon smartly; and, when it becomes necessary, product recall is effected quickly and with appropriate publicity. In addition to meeting the basic legal requirement that all 'goods' must be fit for purpose and manufactured to comply with health and safety requirements, the brandowner is expected to respond positively to any failure of the product to meet a reasonable consumer's expectations. The brandowner's after-sales obligation is normally limited to the initial purchaser and, in appropriate circumstances, to other economic agents that use the quon by licence of the original purchaser during the warranty period. Most cars remain functionally satisfactory for a decade or longer, though the full brandowner warranty usually expires after three years. The brand owner sometimes publicises an emergent failure in a model long after the expiry of the warranty period, as a cost of maintaining the image of the brand to support future sales. Some brands – notably of medicines and of foodstuffs – are explicitly *not* guaranteed after the clearly stated 'use by' or 'best before' date that is shown on the packaging; and suppliers such as retail pharmacists offer facilities for disposal of out-of-date quons that could become dangerous or be misused.

The demand for a brand – particularly some classes of durable quons - can significantly be increased when there is an option to hire rather than buy the consumer experience. Many authorities have suggested that leasing consumption experiences, rather than buying durable quons, will be a defining feature of sophisticated consumerism in this century. A firm of lift manufacturers can lease 'vertical transportation' to the residents of a block of apartments, rather than sell a lift to the builder. The provider installs, maintains and periodically updates the lift; charging the occupants a regularly recalibrated rental that can take account of inflation, of increasing costs arising from changing technology or regulatory change, and of the developing expectations of users of elevators. Under this type of contract the users can always have a state of the art vertical transportation experience. Hiring a quon shifts the focus of the initial transaction away from an expression of the potential buyer's capability to raise a cash price at a specific date onto the predicted capacity of the lessee's income stream to bear the rental payments that will continue throughout the contract period. Over the period of such a lease, lessees must meet the cost of the lessor's capital, and the costs of brand defence and product development, within the hire charge. This principle applies to the billions of pounds' worth of quonic capital equipment that is leased throughout industry and commerce, as much as it does to consumer quons hired by households.

Differential hire charges for similar quonic experiences, facilities or services reflect differentiation in product design, quality of service, brand reputation, snob appeal, material robustness of the components and other characteristics which vary in importance through time and across categories of products and services. The relative importance of the various criteria is determined by consumer expectations. Some brandowners – for example, in healthcare equipment and sophisticated printing technology - refuse to sell the equipment that they build: they insist on leasing agreements which stipulate that they must control specified maintenance services; hoping to inhibit piracy of their *ik* by not equipping users of their output with manuals from which technical secrets could be captured.

No branded quon can be kept on the market for a sustained period if the proportion of its ultimate retail price that is received by the brandowner does not cover the full costs of creating and protecting the brand, including:

- Reputation;
- Patents;
- Brand names;
- Marque and product type names within the brand;
- Logos;
- Trademarks;
- Copyright descriptive writing;
- Copyright images;
- Designs;
- Marketing research;
- Marketing: including advertising and 'Corporate Social Responsibility';
- Contract terms, including warranties, guarantees and limits to liability;
- Methods of securing revenue that are most convenient to the purchaser;
- Pursuit of makers and sellers of fakes, including prosecution and publicity;
- Management of the media to prevent or refute 'knocking' stories;
- General publicity to maintain and enhance favourable brand awareness;
- After-sales service;
- Provision of complementary products [filters, cleaning materials etc] without which the equipment cannot work effectively;
- Replacement of 'unsatisfactory' units under warranty;
- Effective user-friendly complaint and customer query handling;
- Capability to meet clients' liability demands;
- Assurance of environmental acceptability.

Some of the costs of establishing these attributes predate the assembly of the components of individual units of the product, and others arise at or after the time when the ownership or lease of the quon has been added to the asset register of the consumer's estate. Some costs arise directly from the differential performance of individual units in the hands of diverse consumers, while others of the above heads of expenditure serve the general promotion of the brand over several years and sometimes across a range of *marques*.

Price differentials are not the major criterion for choice between brands that lie within any segment of a highly stratified market, in the mind of a consumer who intends to buy a quon and has decided broadly how much they can afford to pay. Image, design, social *cachet*, reputation for reliability and a host of other non-price factors exert huge influence on the consumer's selection between the competing brands. The brandowner offers the quon to distributors at an indicative wholesale price [often as a basis for negotiation with retailers] in each currency zone, within a total tariff 'basket' that is designed to provide sufficient aggregate income for the firm to make a profit from global sales of this quon, after meeting:

- the after-sales costs that may arise in this year relating to units of the brand that were sold in past years and are still in use;
- the costs of manufacturing, logistics and warehousing material products [including cassettes and other media for distributing some immaterial quons] in this year,
- the costs of marketing and selling the items that are to be sold in this year,
- the costs incurred in protecting the brand's *ik* from pirates and detractors, and any costs arising from doing deals with unsavoury or corrupt regimes,
- and this year's spending on developments for the future.

A firm that operates manufacturing and distribution facilities in a dozen countries and supplies customers in more than a hundred and fifty sovereign states, each with their own taxation and regulatory regimes [which are often further complicated by state and local taxes, inspectorates and bylaws], faces a mass of political, currency and tax risks; as well as the risks that are posed by the natural environment, by any process plant that they control, by the variability of the materials and of the workforce; and by the costs that arise from the after-sales expectations of the consumers. All these factors create differentials in the local shop price that is set for any branded quon in different parts of the global distribution system.

Each intending buyer is free to check out the range of available alternative purchase possibilities within the accessible market before making a decision on which segment to enter, then determining which brand to buy. A middle-sized family saloon car is not competing with stretched limos or with Chelsea 4X4s, or with minimalist runabouts. The competitors within the family car segment of the market comprise other brands of middle-market hatchback saloon. Similar considerations apply to customer selections of computer games or downloaded video or audio. Each buyer makes a selection from the models that are offered within the accessible segment; taking account of the complementary costs arising from the purchase, notably fuel and insurance in the case of motor vehicles.

Any firm or individual that controls a quonic brand, even in a highly competitive mass market segment, cherishes a *mini-monopoly* over its registered brand name and over the copyright to its advertising slogans and trademarks, and over any relevant patents or copyrights that it owns; and in all the other significant areas of *ik* that it commands. It seeks the maximum possible differentiation from other brands, both subjectively in the consumer's perception and objectively in the array of protection that the firm acquires and asserts for its *ik*. In the special cases of high fashion clothing and of some ephemeral accessories, items can retain their brand labels when they are released in end-of-season sales for a fraction of the price that was quoted when the design was launched. This dramatic price periodicity does not harm the brands because the ephemeral nature of fashion is fully understood, and highly competent consumers' attention is focused on the *ik* that inheres in the next new season's designs. This pricing strategy is not replicable in the majority of the other segments of the pattern of quonic demand and supply.

In many quonic market segments it is more efficient to protect the *ik* that has been invested in a model by dismantling unsold units and re-using the fungible components; rather than to let recognisable output become available at a discounted price in some secondary market place where it can potentially undermine the *cachet* of the entire brand. Factory shops enable some businesses to sell 'surplus' stock and 'seconds' whose components cannot be disassembled for incorporation in new branded produce. The rapid transmission of information on the internet makes informal offloading of any surplus stock – especially of a durable quon - even more risky for brand reputation now than it was in past generations. A landmark case in France in the middle of 2008 concluded that brandowners are entitled to compensation from a trader or a trading platform that facilitates sales of fakes of their quons; thus extending the range of protection to the *ik* in a brand.

Owners of highly desired luxury brands of material commodities must be careful about making any decision to increase output to meet rising demand, lest they find that the market falls away after a short-term surge in sales. The image of a top-of-the-range brand would not be enhanced if a significantly increased supply of the quon was put on the market at a reduced price. Such a change would probably be perceived to have devalued the decisions of existing consumers who had paid the previous, higher price. From the firm's point of view, it is irrational to decrease the inward cash flow per unit sold that was previously available to cover risks to *ik*, to develop new *ik*, and to diminish the profitability of the brand, in order to gain a cohort of less wealthy customers who may make greater demands for after-sales service; and whose use of the brand might further tarnish the image of the product in the eyes of higher net worth people. These strictures do not necessarily apply when the price is lowered sensitively to dispose quickly of the residual stock of a marque or a model that is being discontinued.

Competitive downward price adjustment can be effective in specific short-term circumstances: for example, if the objective is to finish-off a competitor in a market segment where demand is limited, or is declining. Directors of brandowning firms consider the possibility of merging with other brandowners, or attempting a preemptive acquisition of a competitor, when brands are facing new sources of competition, or when the consumer experience is passing out of fashion; or because of the approaching expiry date of crucial patents or of other time-limited *ik*; or because input materials are becoming inaccessible, or because some phase of the production process – or the product itself – is becoming unsustainable on environmental or public health grounds. Firms that own obsolescent brands commonly carry legacy expenses, including:

- pensions obligations, including commitments to ex-employees who have retired or moved on to other jobs while retaining deferred benefits;
- uninsured employer's liabilities to present and past employees;
- uninsured environmental liabilities for pollution around the sites of factories that may already have been sold or demolished;
- potential after-sales service demands from customers, some of which relate to brands and products that have been discontinued but nevertheless bear an ongoing contractual obligation for a successor brandowner to manufacture spare parts or complementary products such as filters;
- potential contingent liabilities to counterparties.
- potential liabilities to past and present customers;
- costs of maintaining the integrity of the firm's accumulated *ik*, which may include valuable residual assets that were formerly incorporated in quons that are no longer on sale.

One scheme for trying to achieve long-term corporate viability, which was at its most fashionable in the early to mid-nineteen-nineties, was to create *conglomerates*. A 'holding company' bought a range of firms that controlled an array of dissimilar brands in different market sectors. Proponents argued that the resulting ragbag of disparate marcoms and quons that the firm produced from widely spread factories could be distributed more efficiently to buyers from rationalised warehousing systems, or sold direct to consumers from unified product catalogues. These hopes generally proved to be exaggerated; though some past failures may have succeeded in the present state of on-line trading. The multifarious manufacturing plant were often located where former owners of the brands had been able to claim the biggest industrial development grants in some past era, which in changed times incur unnecessarily complex logistical costs. Conglomerates typically increased their gearing to finance each successive takeover, so they could not quickly invest enough additional capital in their acquisitions to rationalise manufacturing or warehousing onto consolidated sites; or to invest in new *ik*.

A conglomerate also had to meet all the defence and developmental costs attaching to the *ik* that was integral to the brands that it wanted to maintain or develop. To reduce this costly tangle of problems, some conglomerates sold viable brands that could be designated 'non-core' businesses. The firm that buys ownership of such a brand takes possession of the complex of *ik* that is identifiable as the source of demand for that brand. Fees are paid to advisors to undertake all the 'due diligence' that is needed to ensure that the buyer of a brand takes control of the requisite plant and machinery, the key people and the *ik* that they require: and nothing more. The conglomerate that divests itself of the brand is left carrying the *kos* that have been incurred in preserving the brand up to the date of sale, and the costs of slimming down the firm's infrastructure into the shape that the new owner is willing to buy. Hence a typical demerger carries vendor costs for redundancies and written-off of debt; as well as the cost of the heritage obligations. A similar transference of a set of business assets can be effected, without carrying the company's debt burden, when a 'pre-packaged liquidation' is arranged

The record of mergers and corporate acquisitions [M&A] shows that, in general and especially in mature sectors of the economy, post-merger profits do not improve upon the profits that were record by the component firms as they had been before the merger. Banks, accountants and law firms draw huge fees from facilitating corporate mergers, and those payments constitute a drain of wealth out of the 'real economy' into the financial services sector. Even the most successful mergers produce organisations that are significantly less than a full combination of the former components. Similarly, many very highly leveraged buyouts of companies by speculative venture capital incur financing costs that can partly be serviced by raising prices, but this can soon meet with sales resistance from retailers or from their customers. The most obvious means to increase short-term profits is to 'strip out cost' from the business, and almost always such 'surgery' has a detrimental impact on the firm's ability to defend and develop *ik*; but this is not a significant concern to a short-term speculator who intends to sell the business before the spending cuts cause perceptible diminution of the desirability of the brand or of the efficiency of the plant.

Beneficial mergers and acquisitions occur most naturally where demand is growing rapidly for brands that incorporate a new technology or a new consumer concept and are creating a new market segment. In those conditions the more aggressive firms in the sector absorb their rivals to gain control of those companies' *ik* and market share and productive capacity. In recent years this has been particularly marked in the fields of information technology, on-line games and pharmaceuticals: but the recent history of *Hewlet Packard* is a spectacular example of such a strategy that has repeatedly soured. Aside from the special cases of emergent markets and novel quons, M&A activity is often an indicator of sectorial decline. Thus one can expect that facilitating defensive M&A, especially in Europe, will provide revenue for bankers and lawyers throughout the coming decade, as global competition slices away the historically cosy markets that European brandowners have enjoyed. We will also see a continuance of the purchase of US and European companies for control of their *ik* by firms based in India, China and other emergent economies

Understanding the factors that cause favoured brands to be most preferred by buyers is important in assessing the utility of *ik* to brandowners; and the contribution of *ik* to the pricing of shares in a firm. Psychological research on consumers' perceptions, backed by an improving scientific understanding of the biology, chemistry and electrically measurable activity of the human brain, indicates that brand recognition occurs in the egocentric and image-conscious right-side frontal area. Choices that respond to activity in this region of the brain are highly significant to people, and it is apparent that individuals invest emotional energy in the pride of ownership and in the sensation of luxury that comes from using preferred quons. It is also increasingly clear that the 'hard wiring' of the brain is not completed until the very late teens; so younger people cannot be assumed to have perceptions or preferences that are similar to those of mature adults. Because they are addressing these prominent forces in human nature, the cost centres within a brandowning firm that address the psychologically sensitive aspects of consumer relations such as design, marketing, image protection and after-sales service – and, latterly, green credentials and maybe even a claim of corporate social responsibility - can demand an amount of the attention of the chief executive that greatly exceeds the time allocated to manufacturing cost centre managers.

Some of the most highly desired brands cover physical products that are materially less robust, less durable, and less finely styled than some of their competitors; and some of the most highly-reputed services are far from the most perfect available: but yet the most financially capable celebrity customers demand to have those most-preferred brands for reputational and emotional reasons. The millions of daily demonstrations of this blatant and persistent refusal by consumers to act 'rationally' are a further proof of the practical irrelevance of pristine academic Economics. So-called Behavioural Economics attempts to explain aspects of reality alongside the formulaic mainstream of the subject; and it could become useful if its practitioners freed themselves from the redundant intellectual impedimenta that they continue to tolerate

Psychological and social mechanisms determine the quonic desirability of a brand and indicate the utility that a potential consumer attributes to that experience. The need to preserve and, whenever possible, to enhance the benefit that the consumer gets from the quon compels the owner of the brand to accept the increasing *ik*-related costs of achieving synergy with the aspirations of egocentric human consumers. A brandowner's failure to deliver the product or the experience on time in the desired quantity might in some cases cause the customer to want the quon with more passion than before. Some individuals may accept gracefully the excuse for short-term non-performance that the supplier proffers. Alternatively – as in any matter where emotions are engaged – the consumer might turn away from the pursuit of that experience to look for an alternative source of satisfaction.

In each market segment in which he or she has a quonic consumer aspiration, the individual aims to secure the brand that will provide them with the highest level of satisfaction that they can afford; in the context of their spending power [including available loan finance] and of their preferences. Firms carefully assess the potential efficacy and profitability of alternative branded offerings of equipment and machinery, workspace construction methods and a huge range of investments; including service providers from lawyers to coffee-machine leasing firms. Brand marketing aims to achieve the perceptual segregation of the consumer experience by users of that brand; and the brandowner must ensure that the means of delivering that consumer experience are constantly fit-for-purpose. The most preferred quons are enjoyed in a context of mutual self-interest. Consumers collude with brandowners to protect the exclusivity of the *ik* that consumers have accessed, and in so doing they promote the brand. Keeping a durable quon in a pristine state for its 'product lifetime' is more often assured by the actions of the consumer than of the supplier; however tightly drawn might be the after-sales service requirements on the supplier, or the maintenance conditions that are imposed in a lease of a consumer experience.

Almost all foodstuffs that are available in advanced countries are now subject to close regulation – exemplified in animal 'passports', certificates of origin of fruit etc – and consequently in cases where those products are not branded the retailer must take responsibility for the chain of certification. Providing such assurance for the consumer is a very significant feature of contemporary retailing; and the cost of this provision is usually split between the retailer and the brandowner. In west Europe this regime was threatened by the scandal that erupted early in 2013 when horse meat was found in 'beef' meals and pork was identified in 'halal' meals in some supermarkets. The recovery process required much more rigour in the verification of authenticity of ingredients. This scandal gave an unexpected impetus to a process that began in the supply of milk in the UK. For a long period farmers received barely the cost of production of fresh milk at the farm gate, and were for several years at a loss to understand where the mark-up was generated that enabled the supermarkets to sell the same commodity profitably. From the consumer perspective, labelling and certification make packets of milk acceptably quonic. Wily farmers understood that mechanism before the favourable 'correction' in commodity prices moved in their favour after 2008. They now make a good return on the part of their output that they can sell as their own-label products and by using Farmers' Markets, where increasingly rigorous measures are enforced to ensure that participants stick to the 'own produce only' rule to preserve the added utility of the generic *Farmers' Market* brand which has become a powerful neoquon. The food adulteration scandal made local certification of origin of food very attractive to the public, and farmers' markets and local butchers [sourcing their meat locally] received a new boost to their success.

In the sophisticated cities of the most advanced countries market stalls, pound shops and cut-price stores sell surplus stocks of 'deleted' branded goods and a range of marcoms that meet the legislative requirements to be 'fit for purpose'. There is also a significant 'under-the-counter' trade in marcoms for which no trader will accept liability, and in pirate videos and audio cassettes that evade the copyright protection system. Some openly sold marcoms bear a maker's mark, but that does not denote a brand that the consumer would wish to announce that he owned: though such a mark may well indicate the maker's desire to build his product into a brand. A broom or a hammer that is bought as a marcom from a market stall can be as effective for its purpose as a much higher-priced quon that performs the same function; but in the absence of the verifiable range of *ik* that is inherent in a quon, the commodity is priced as a marcom. It is highly probable that – alongside the emergence of secondary brands - more marcom production for direct human consumption will become viable in the postindustrial countries as real wages fall: and thus, to some extent, they will become reindustrialised.

The idea of a *consumer's surplus* applies most obviously when a consumer has the choice between buying a well-regarded branded refrigerator [for example] for £800 and a neoquon of similar appearance and capacity at £250, plus an optional £40 for an extended warranty. The consumer who opts for the neoquon foregoes the experience of being a premium quon consumer in that arena, but he has a *consumer's surplus* of £510 [or, if he dispenses with the extended warranty, £550] to spend on other things. Alternatively £550 can be seen as the *opportunity-cost* to the consumer who pays the higher price for accessing the intangible benefits that attach to buying the quon. Purchasing quons at reduced prices in a sale, or importing them from a country with a different taxation regime, without dilution of after-sales service from the brandowner, also generates a consumer's surplus; usually at the cost of significant time spent by the buyer on effecting the purchase and on the pursuit of any after-sales benefit in cases of personal imports from abroad.

Individuals who have utilitarian requirements for durable goods, but cannot afford [or choose not] to buy either quons or neoquons, can enter the second-hand market in search of cars and electrical equipment, pushchairs, furniture, and a range of other durables; even including clothing. No contractual brandowner obligations attach to the material residue of former quons and neoquons that are resold as [specifically non-jevic] 'second-hand' items, especially after the terminal date of the makers' acceptance of responsibility for product liability. Nor do retailers accept any responsibility for the utility or safety of neoquons that they once sold, beyond the expiry date of any warranty that they sold as part of the original deal. A wise second-hand trader sells items 'as seen' and leaves all the more risky elements of such trade – and all the dodgy items - to be offered for private sale in the small ads columns of local newspapers, on corner shop notice boards, and in their internet equivalents.

For several centuries a vast array of products has been made specifically for use by the armed forces, to be purchased on a basis of quasi-quonic pricing. The design of a device may be owned by the Admiralty or the Ministry of Defence, in which case the manufacture can be franchised out to the private-sector supplier that submits the most efficient tender in cases where there is no government arsenal, factory or shipyard that is available and competent to perform the task. Alternatively the *ik* may be owned by a corporation that contracts to supply its quon to the government at a negotiated price. During and after the Second World War, a huge range of consumer goods ranging from 'National' orange juice and cod liver oil for infants, through quality-certified margarine and soap, to 'utility' clothing and furniture was distributed to the general population under the control of government agencies; in rationed quantities at controlled prices. In the event of a non-nuclear global war, or following the near-collapse of the economy in an extreme future depression, a similar system could be reintroduced to distribute a minimum *per capita* supply of subsistence goods through a rationing system. Such a command economy is necessarily bureaucratic, inefficient and regressive; and it could bring about temporary stagnation in the generation of *ik*: but it could keep many people alive for a considerable period in crisis conditions.

Devotees of the 'efficient market' dogma urged governments to enforce *competition* – by decree - even in areas of *natural monopoly*, where the infrastructure can only safely and efficiently be administered by a single management and where the cost of duplicating or triplicating infrastructure is absurd waste. In Britain by 1980 the main utilities – gas, electricity, coalmining, and the railways - had been brought into state ownership under successive administrations; other services, notably telephones and television, had been developed under state and municipal ownership. The Tories had been content to keep them in the public sector through the nineteen sixties; and the nationalisation of water sources was enacted by the Heath government in the seventies. The pace of investment in capacity and infrastructure, and the prices that were charged by state-owned utilities and industries, could be manipulated: unstated social tariffs could ensure the affordability of utilities to vulnerable customers; and managed wholesale pricing could create an inconspicuous subsidy to selected industrial customers, not least to the other nationalised industries. Research and development, and investment in new plant and infrastructure, could be phased to minimise the impact on them of fluctuations in the economic cycle. Sometimes nationalised industries returned a surplus to the state, sometimes they received state assistance.

Regardless of whether water supply is a state monopoly, a private monopoly or has competing private providers, population growth and the intensification of human economic activity have driven water tables deeper and made clean surface water resources scarcer in India, in the Sahel, in southeast England, in much of China and of Australia, and at hundreds of other stress points around the globe. Climatic variation has exacerbated drought in several significant regions. Most British people have grown up thinking of water as a 'free good' that is provided by nature and accessed as a public service; but in reality for many centuries quality-controlled safe water – if it has been available at all - has been sold. Potable water delivered to the tap is a quon; and almost everywhere the cost of delivering it is increasing inexorably. Water that falls as rain and snow in parts of urban areas where it cannot sink naturally into the ground must either be harvested or subject to managed removal, often in combination with waste water and sewerage. No community can for long evade responding to the fact that acceptable standards of public health and community hygiene come at a significant cost that will increase with demographic trends, urbanisation and climate change.

People's tastes shift with product development. New technology and innovation in the media and leisure sectors generate a constantly expanding array of potential consumer choices. Older generations express genuine astonishment that most children and many young men adults spend most of their waking hours 'playing' with their favourite fashionable packages on their smart devices. Demand for the experiences that are provided in some segments of the leisure market increases from day to day; while in other sectors demand declines as the brands' designs and technologies are perceived to be obsolescent. This extends to phenomena such as the intensification of exploitation of the world's most famous football teams: which are both enabled and forced to acquire and pay large squads of young men with very scarce talents in order to keep within an increasingly complex schedule of competitions. Firms in most quonic sectors are challenged to keep the development of their *ik*, and their promotional strategy, ahead of the changing pattern of demand; not least in acknowledgement of pressure on terrestrial resources and rising awareness of the possible benefits and massive costs of the green agenda.

For the past half-century pharmaceutical companies have been pressed to release cut-price bulk supplies of *generic* versions of their patented drugs for use by state hospitals in the advanced countries. Some patent-holders are put under pressure to permit the *ik* on their drugs to be used by other firms and agencies, who can make a cut-price version for state agencies. This principle has been extended to induce pharmaceutical firms to supply their products to less-developed countries at significantly less than their normal quonic market price. Some governments have threatened to remove protection from producers' *ik* unless they make generic supplies of their drugs available on 'special terms', for the state health service or to deliver more benefit from their spending on international aid. Some marxist and marginalist Economists see such outcomes as a step towards their *nirvana* of 'marginal cost pricing': that is, forcing firms to set prices that allow no return for the creation and preservation of *ik*; which would make capitalist innovation unaffordable. The removal of 'profit' from firms' income would mean that they had no funds to combat agencies in emergent economies that chose to pirate their *ik*. In such a world dictators could support the theft of *ik* and the proceeds from their exports of pirated produce would pile up in the kleptocrats' Swiss bank accounts.

One mechanism to address this dilemma is to develop variants of proven drugs specifically for manufacture and distribution in less-developed countries; particularly for endemic diseases that could become more common in the postindustrial countries as mass migration continues. Mega-rich individuals have taken a lead in some such areas by investing in treatment programmes, and several 'first-world' governments have used portions of their overseas aid programmes for the same purpose. It is questionable whether the concept can be extended beyond healthcare and the provision of simple information and communications technology in the near future.

# CHAPTER FIVE

# PRODUCTIVENESS, PRODUCTIVITY AND INCOMES

Some highly regarded philosophers and Political Economists have speculated as to whether human life could be 'better' if people lived without coercive organisations or laws to protect property, as appeared to be the case with *aboriginal* peoples in Australia and the Kalahari Desert when European explorers first 'discovered' them. The situation of such peoples was described – even idealised – as 'primitive communism' in which each person was assumed to draw on the 'bounty of nature' to meet simple subsistence requirements. On deeper examination, anthropologists found that the hunter-gatherers had complex structures for resolving or preventing interpersonal and intergenerational conflict, for the selection of breeding partners, for excluding strangers from their clans; for personal ornament, for religious observance and for the treatment of perceived illnesses [both mental and physical]. It also became obvious that many such people willingly escape from traditional social and economic structures as soon as there is the chance of securing a waged job that will give them access to quonic consumption. Given this facet of human nature, the existence of a government is consensually accepted on the grounds that *ik* - and thus quons, and the possession of quons - cannot exist without the law of property, which is a major component of the rule of law that only a state - a *polis* - can provide.

In all relatively affluent societies consumers have shown an increasingly strong preference to buy access to experiences that incorporate more attractive *ik*, including wholly immaterial quons that are accessed electronically, rather than simply acquiring more material things. This tendency was represented by the sophistication of drama [and of theatre construction] and of games in classical Greece, by advances in astronomy in China and around the Mediterranean and in the refinement of prayer and meditation that has been achieved by minorities in many cultures in monasteries and other special mind-focusing centres. There have also been cases of extreme decadence, as in the phase of Roman society that was damned by St Augustine. The present incidence of obesity in the formerly industrial countries demonstrates that sophisticated and sensible preferences are not always followed, even among the most economically and socially advantaged populations in world history. After allowing for such glaring exceptions, the shift from marcom to quon consumption, and changing patterns of demand for quons, confirm a remarkable 'greening' of consumer choice: though the ubiquity of pornography on the internet, blighted by increasing extremity of child abuse, presents clearly the ambiguity of such resources.

The perception that capable consumers prefer to receive the 'necessities, comforts and conveniences of life' in the form of what this text calls quons, rather than as marcoms, has a long history. By the year seventeen hundred, European Political Economists had agreed that three indispensable *factors of production* were required to provide any marketed wares:

- *capital:* the necessary equipment to convert raw materials into the objects that people want to consume, and are willing to pay for; plus a cash float to enable suppliers to buy the necessary input materials, machinery, labour and licenses;
- *land:* the source of the materials that are extracted from or cultivated on the earth in the forms of crops, timber, animals, minerals and water;
- *labour:* the intellectual and physical capabilities of human beings to produce things and experiences that they and others needs and desire; using capital in association with materials that are extracted from the land, as appropriate.

That construct was dramatically recalibrated during the eighteenth century. The fecundity of the human race in creating ideas that can be applied in material production was also released so that it increased human satisfaction through entertainment and cultural activity. Professional management as well as greater professionalism by producers and performers was developed in the plastic arts, in architecture, in publishing, in music and on the stage. Haydn was brought to London by an entrepreneurial publisher, whose concert promotions brought the composer wealth beyond his previous imagination. Mozart and Beethoven both composed concertos primarily to display their virtuosity as pianists; but they also composed pieces for others to perform, usually in response to paid commissions, in which they sold the right to perform the intellectual creation whilst they retained a right of attribution as the creator. This was parallel to the sale of **access to** intellectual property by the great inventive patent holders, James Watt, Matthew Boulton, Josiah Wedgwood and Richard Arkwright. When Adam Smith wrote about the 'division of labour' he reported on a dying tradition. His observation of the famous pin factory showed that different men specialised in providing physical prowess, manual dexterity and each an understanding of his contribution to the process [and of the materials and of the tools with which he was an expert]; which had the effect that the team of specialists had a much higher productivity as a collective than would have been achieved by each man doing all of the jobs. As was his wont, Smith elevated this into a universal principle: which was already nonsense by the day his book was published, because by then Arkwright had demonstrated a massive increase in the **productiveness** of his patented plant as compared with the hand-powered [or foot-powered], manually-fed spinning wheel.

The division of labour showed that a complex manufacturing task could be broken down into a sequence of relatively simple operations; which could then be mechanised. With the introduction of modern machines an exponentially greater level of productivity was achieved by the application of a patent combined with a significant capital input. This meant that the output produced per penny of wages paid to the employees increased spectacularly. Smith's beautifully ordered world of handicraftsmen becoming ever-more specialist to carry forward the division of labour until its product reached the limit of the market was trumped by disruptive technologies combined with abundant capital. Smith's 'principle' of the division of labour is still trotted out in some basic Economics classes, and the three 'factors of production' also get a mention, sometimes with 'entrepreneurship' tentatively been offered as a potential fourth factor. But *ik* has for over two centuries been too powerful a reality for Economists to incorporate in their superficially clever models: the driving force behind most innovation in the contemporary world and the sphere of activity that consumers get most excited about has not been accommodated.

The trades unions were first established to protect the interests of skilled handworkers: some of whose jobs were threatened by the very first of the new textile machines. After the defeat of the despairing attempt by the Luddites to smash up the new machinery the unions swiftly adapted to focus on the skilled minority of the post-Arkwright workforce who built, installed and maintained the machinery that the new unskilled mass of factory workers operated. Attempts to unionise the mass of the unskilled were never successful; but groups like miners who were exposed to special risks were able to build credible unions because their threat to shut down their workplaces would cause major disruption of the whole economy. Throughout the industrial era the intelligent majority of British and American trade union leaders have recognised that their members choose to spend their freely-earned wages on a range of choices – tobacco, alcohol, betting shops, traditional foods and sweets, patent medicaments and popular entertainment – that no Marxist would regard as 'needs'. This explains both why democratic trade unionism had never been captured by communists who do not recognise *ik*; and why the unions were broadly supportive of keynesian policy after the Second World War.

It is unnecessary to follow the evolution of either industry or labour organisations from 1800 to the present millennium, beyond noting that the visible structure of industry and the subtle constructs of society have throughout that time been fundamentally different from the structures that Adam Smith had in mind when he established the propositions that still exercise their malign influence in Economics; and through Economics they pervert policy.

To the great benefit of the human species a towering genius appeared in the first half of the twentieth century; though neither his contemporaries nor his followers have quite understood the important and probably unintended consequences of his influence on the subsequent economy. John Maynard Keynes is quite unique among writers on the economy. Extensive reference has already been made to him both as a promoter of practical solutions to the economic issues of his day and as an innovative thinker who clearly described the asset class called keyns in this text. When he constructed his *General Theory of Employment, Interest and Money [1936]*, Keynes took marginalist microeconomics as 'given': and essentially irrelevant. Working from the polar opposite of normative Economics, Keynes presented an understanding of the total economy as one gigantic mechanism. He postulated that the aggregate performance of all the agents active in the economy could be improved as a result of government intervention in the enveloping system that was to become known as the macroeconomy. His starting point was that politically dangerous levels of unemployment – such as had occurred in Europe and North America in the nineteen thirties – were the consequences of a deficiency of *effective demand* for the output that the economy could produce. *Aggregate demand* was understood to consist broadly of what was spent within the economy on two elements:

> *consumption* [**C**: purchases of consumer goods] both by households and by corporate entities including public sector agencies; and
> *investment* [**I**: purchases of producers' goods and infrastructure investments] predominantly by firms and by public sector agencies.

Keynes assumed that the overall economic activity of a government that maintained a balanced budget would neither add to nor to diminish the total of consumption and investment **(C + I)**. This assumes that the state collected taxes, licence fees and other dues from organisations and individuals, and spent all that money within the same accounting period on its own consumption and investment. But if the government received some revenue and did not spend it, the result was that potential demand in the economy was reduced by the amount of state revenue that was unspent: in such a case, *aggregate demand* would be:

$$[C + I] - G$$

- **C** is spending by all economic persons and entities [including central and local government and state agencies] on consumption of goods and services within the accounting period,
- **I** is spending on investment goods and services by both the public and private sectors during the period,
- **G** is the amount of revenue that the government withheld from spending.

But if **G** were to be made **positive**, if the government's spending into the economy [C+I+G] was more than it took out of the system in taxes and other charges, that net additional spending could create demands that would cause unemployed people and underemployed resources to be brought into use. A bold government could issue orders for equipment, and pay export credits or industrial development grants to firms; and it could employ men and women directly as nurses or teachers; or on road building and other public works. The net new government spending would have a *multiplier effect* as it was passed through the economy, and the autonomous economic growth that would follow from each injection of extra purchasing-power into an under-employed economy would empower newly-employed [or re-deployed] people to buy more consumer goods; and enable the firms that produced those goods to invest in improved facilities, services and products. If the government part-funded the spending programme by borrowing, buyers of the new government debt – notably pension and life assurance funds – would accrue income-yielding *ka*s in their portfolios. The interest due to be paid on those *ka*s and their eventual redemption by the state would be funded by the additional taxes that could be levied on the expanded economy.

After the Second World War the Marxist International presented a real threat to democracy, with the Soviet Union claiming to be creating a workers' paradise while home-grown communists exerted subversive influence, using trade unions where that was practicable. Macroeconomists who styled themselves keynesians proposed that in any period when aggregate output [an estimate of the total that was spent on transactions] was not growing sufficiently to meet a target set by the government, the sorts of intervention that had been proposed by Keynes to stimulate the system to greater activity should be deployed. Twin reasons were cited for the need to apply keynesian techniques: first, the population continued to increase: consequently the government should create a macroeconomic context that would provide opportunities for more employment. Secondly, at successive elections politicians promised that their proposed policies would raise the standard of living for the population. This proposition became inextricably linked to an assumption that only a 'fully employed' economy would generate sufficient tax revenues to pay for law and order, and for defence, and for the welfare state.

Tragically, from the middle nineteen-fifties onward governments were under pressure from Economists to implement their agenda of creating the environment for competition in 'efficient' markets. Though Keynes usually spoke it softly he made it clear [for example in the proceedings of the Macmillan Committee in the late nineteen-twenties] that the sort of policies that he was to advocate required the state and the banks to work together in selecting which industrial sectors should be favoured for investment; and it was clearly implicit that the investments, once committed, should be carried through to completion. By contrast Economists asserted that firms were fully autonomous and therefore they must determine their investment and product development strategies alone, in competition with other firms. Thus while the economic environment around firms was hugely influenced by the shifts of macroeconomic policy, there was no carry-over to ensure that projected investments could be completed through the vicissitudes of tight and relaxed macroeconomic policy. The clumsy alternation of stimulus with squeeze through which post-Keynes 'keynesianism' was enacted, caused firms to respond to each squeeze on the system by reducing or cancelling projects and investments. Every time the government and the Bank of England applied a stimulus to the economy by reducing taxes, releasing spending-power and lowering interest rates [to make corporate and personal borrowing easier], the cash flowed immediately into consumers' pockets and increasingly-responsive retail businesses financed the stocking of more imported consumer goods for the consumers. New British manufacturing capacity would take years to construct, before which the investment could have been aborted in the next credit squeeze. Some development of capacity did take place, especially in making innovative products and those with strong and secure brands; but it was not enough to carry the whole economy to new heights. Hence the most significant response to economic stimulus was more imports, at the same time as domestic consumers increased their demand for British goods. Factory orders from the home market were given priority, which resulted in a decline [or, at best, a reduction in the rate of increase] of export earnings. So a balance of payments crisis appeared and the government had to apply a severe squeeze on the economy to prevent a collapse of the currency in global exchanges.

Between 1950 and 1980 successive governments in the UK, as in several other European countries, tried to develop the welfare state whilst also using keynesian means to stimulate employment and aggregate demand in the economy. The taxation necessary to fund the welfare system made British goods dearer both at home and in export markets while British firms met increasing competition from suppliers of branded quons in Europe, North America, Japan, and then in Korea; which had a serious negative impact on the balance of payments. Britain's dependency on imported oil became especially burdensome after the 1973 price hike by the OPEC countries; but there was no policy to return to dependency on coal as the principal source of energy in an era when individual motor transport was seen as a major component of a high living standard. The overexposure of the British economy to imports led to the sterling crisis of 1976-7 that could only be resolved by taking a loan from the International Monetary Fund on terms that required a reduction in the rate of increase in public spending in future years. But even Margaret Thatcher's governments, which came into office in 1979, could not eradicate the country's addiction to over-spending. The Conservatives were keen to buy votes by reducing taxes. They believed that lower taxation would support economic growth, and that tax revenues would rise in due course. To provide a temporary source of funds for the Treasury to spend on defence, education, benefits and the health service, state-owned industries and services were privatised in the nineteen-eighties and thereafter. The government sold assets that had cost taxpayers many billions of pounds, at prices that look in retrospect to have been excessively modest. The money that was received from these sales was not used to fund the next generation of productive investment or to create a sovereign wealth fund; it was blown in short-term spending that the government could not otherwise have afforded. No government adequately assessed the contribution that could be earned from the current and potential holdings of *ik* within the entities that were privatised

Military and naval installations, school sports fields, government buildings and hospital sites were sold: some were asserted to be 'surplus to requirements' but others, incredibly, were sold for leaseback by the state. Future scholars will be incredulous that the disposals list included key utilities and basic industries: coal, steel, water, gas, electricity, airlines and airports; and firms with globally relevant *ik*: *Rolls-Royce, BP, ICL, BT, Cable&Wireless, Westinghouse* [a leader in nuclear power generation and the construction of nuclear generation plant], massive holdings of real estate, and a range of scientific research establishments. The most conspicuous instance of all-party serial incompetence was the privatisation and subsequent regulation of the railways. Some sectors of business that were privatised have obviously thrived outside the public sector: but such a rush to sell businesses and key public utilities without sensible appreciation of their potential to generate circulating capital was a disastrous failure of statecraft. The calamity was compounded when the privatised firms were sold on to alien owners, who acquired both valuable *ik* and a perpetual flow of future income from UK consumers.

In preparation for privatisation, sections of state-owned entities that were not considered to be saleable were shut down: including research and development businesses that held significant *ik*, and had the capability to generate more. This crass radicalism also precipitated the failure of innovative independent firms that had been suppliers of specialist equipment and materials to the state organisations. The rapid post-privatisation increase in the prices of shares in the firms that possessed significant *ik* did not caution governments from privatising further state assets on similarly dissolute terms. In general, the prices of quons that were sold by privatised businesses increased year-on-year by more than the published 'rate of inflation'. The privatisation policy was condemned by former [Tory] Prime Minister Harold Macmillan as the equivalent of 'selling the family silver', to enable a spendthrift government to reduce a few taxes and evade increasing others, with scant regard to the future of investment in the country's real economy. Macmillan's comments resonated positively with large sections of the electorate; but had no operational impact on the government as they pressed on with the asset stripping.

As major areas of industry and of the economic infrastructure were privatised, the state abdicated responsibility for allocating capital to research and investment; which had been a significant characteristic of government for over 500 years. Economists asserted that allocation of capital by the state is invariably inefficient; yet under privatisation the replacement model for the generation, collection and allocation of investment capability on railways, power supplies, water supply and telecommunications was to subject capital spending to 'economic regulation'. Ofcom, Ofgem, Ofwat and their peers created a pattern of constraints on enterprise that was in no sense superior to what had happened under state ownership. Decisions affecting essential capital investment became increasingly subject to evasion and delay; as was exemplified in the absence of an investment policy for power supplies that became painfully obvious in 2014. The prospects of electrical power cuts recurring, and of standpipes rationing the domestic water supply, are stronger for the twenty-twenties than at any time since the period of post-second world war reconstruction. The Thatcher-Major-Blair-Brown-Cameron policy continuum did nothing of significance to support new indigenous *ik*-based manufacturing. The implantation of Japanese-owned motor firms redeployed a small proportion of the available skilled labour which 'eighties Britain possessed in abundance; and those works proved over the successive couple of decades that manufacturing could still be highly profitable in the UK. Similar results accrued under Asian ownership to Jaguar-Landrover, which underwent a miraculous turnaround. Meanwhile, almost entirely outside the control or even the notice of the government, the confirmation of English as the undoubted global language was combined with significant private investment in the relevant *ik*, to consolidate Britain's global prominence in cinematography, animation and theatre, computer games, advertising and financial services including sophisticated betting. There is a significant risk that these sectors, which require little fixed plant, will decamp to more amenable jurisdictions if taxation or regulation is perceived to be too burdensome in Britain. Foreign investors have been increasingly willing to buy up UK 'technology' firms in early stages of their growth; and the owners have been willing to sell, especially when British sources of capital are not available to them. Thus the failure of the system to fund productive investment in these firms has alienated the future revenue flows that will be earned by their *ik*.

## Assets as wealth

In both Britain and the USA arcane accounting standards derived from Economics and from the demands of the tax system were imposed on all firms. While they have been effective in enriching the partners in firms of accountants, these rules limit companies' accumulation of strategic reserves to react against threats to their *ik*. Brandowning businesses necessarily maintain pockets of cash that directors have welcomed because the money may periodically be required to meet contingencies that require the immediate deployment of resources to defend the brand and the intellectual property that supports it. An incoming management team that aims simply to extract cash from a business can cut out 'fat', by slimming down costs and liquidating hidden reserves, and can thereby increase short-term returns to the owners. Such tactics are welcomed by the fashionable majority of analysts who agitate for predatory mergers and acquisitions, and encourage takeovers by 'private equity' firms that increase the short-run corporate income stream.

The core 'old-EU' states have hitherto kept their own brands of coffee, electrical household goods, banking, insurance, food retailing, petrol, beer, soap and detergents, furnishings and many other product ranges. These brands have retained predominance in their national markets, despite competition from imports from

the global giants; because they have been protected by linguistic, cultural, regulatory, administrative, sentimental and chauvinistic barriers; which are all
maintained with the vociferous support of trade unions. Such institutions have
hitherto been effectively oblivious to EU integration. The social protection of indigenous brands maintains the productiveness of the investment in the firms that
own the brands. This simple fact explains why reported turnover per employee in
Germany in the twenty-noughties was recorded as being 19% - and in France 22%
- above that recorded for Britain.

Economists' assessment of *productivity* in the USA – the home of brands such
as *Coke* and *Boeing*, *McDonalds* and *Jeep* that can command a premium within their
prices and nevertheless remain competitive – is 39% higher than in Britain. The *ik*
that is embedded in *Microsoft, Google, Dell, IBM, Apple* and many other global leaders in ICT is remunerated at a domicile in the USA: as are the global American news
and entertainment giants, and oil traders, the dominant book publishers and [after
forced restructuring] still the biggest banks. Even more remarkable is the success
of pure intellectual property, developed on line with no material product at all; as
exemplified in *Facebook* and successfully represented by hundreds of successful
games packages and applications. The retention of profits from sales in the USA,
plus repatriation to the USA of the cash that is derived from transfer pricing of the
*ik* that is incorporated in quons that are sold all over the globe, enables American
business to continue to apply the massive concentration of energy in research and
development that has hitherto kept America at the head of the *ik*-reflective league
of productiveness.

Some Economists have recognised the inapplicability of their inherited theory
to quonic prices, and they have tried to construct a measure of the *total factor
productivity* of a firm or of a business sector, adverting to the '*s-factor*'. The *s-factor*
is no mystery, it is the *ik* that is embedded in quons. The earning power of *ik* – the
prices that customers can be cajoled to pay, net of material costs of production,
determines the profitability of brands; and of the retail and distributor brands that
validate neoquons – is quite distinct from the concept of *direct labour productivity*
which provides a monetised assessment of process efficiency in extractive industry
or in manufacturing or in logistics, which can be expressed in wage-hours expended.

The recent flowering of global capitalism has been achieved largely on the basis
of *ik* that was generated in the major powers during the twentieth century, much
of it in government-funded research establishments, later being diffused through
the emergent industrial countries. The democracies are now in danger of experi-
encing a long era of economic regression that is partially derived from a dearth of
investment in new, secret military and space technology. The move of China and
India into the space race has made more conspicuous the retreat of the USA from
that field: and one interesting sub-plot is the growing potential of Britain, France
and Japan as providers of satellite and planetary exploration technologies – principally in firms that can be brought together in consortia – partially backed by

funding from entrepreneurs who have made their fortunes from the control of *ik* in luxury products, in social media and in electronic entertainment. Where it is needed, intellectual support for these projects can usually be obtained from universities; though how long even the best research universities in the UK [and in the wider EU] will be able to maintain their momentum in an era of tightened funding is an open question. A rogue element in this situation is that Chinese, Arab and Indian companies and trusts are keen to buy control of such innovative companies, and the failure of western financial institutions [and of governments] – even to some extent in Germany – to provide the funds for the evolution and growth of the innovators means that more of their *ik* will be alienated, enabling the purchasers to develop the *ik* for their own enrichment.

On a global scale it becomes more painfully obvious that crass dictatorships and failed states prevent their people from reaching first base as consumers of quons, and in the worst cases they drive millions of people into abject destitution. Where there is no capability for individuals to develop and secure *ik*, their economy cannot progress optimally and will most probably regress. Also it is implicit in the preceding paragraph that there is no automatic correlation between party-political democracy and perpetual economic success. Inter-party collusion in shoring up a faltering democracy is no less conducive to economic stagnation than is the rapacity of a third world dictator. In the few dozen countries where the rule of law is genuinely respected, inclusive democracy has been shown to be the best system of government that has yet been devised: but it is not a necessary condition for healthy statehood; and the validated facts of Political Economy are not biased in favour of democracy. Many of the most successful models for the economic management of a state, especially in times when the system must respond to rapid change, have been applied in autocracies, oligarchies, and limited democracies. Tax-and-spend keynesianism served its turn when it bought the consent of a mass electorate during the decades when European democrats deployed a wide range of devices to arm the countries in the North Atlantic Treaty Organisation [NATO] against communism. But after the Soviet Union collapsed, both defence spending [and with it much of the spin-off from research in the form of marketable *ik*] came under challenge as being unaffordable alongside the ever-increasing cost of the welfare state.

In all the postindustrial countries during the past half-century Economists have urged politicians to create macroeconomic conditions that will – supposedly – produce sufficient growth to pay for the welfare state and maintain a thriving competitive economy. The mathematically neat and practically useless theory of 'rational' markets has encouraged the development of patterns of resource allocation that increase government indebtedness year after year and has hitherto enabled current beneficiaries apparently to defy the *Iron Law of Wages*. It has already been stressed that this law is one of the most basic propositions of Political Economy. It states that no economy can rationally allocate more resources to consumption by human beings than that economy produces, *after allocating what is necessary to maintain essential public services and for necessary investment.* The practitioners' insistence on the centrality of the Iron Law was the biggest reason why Political Economy became loathed as 'the dismal science' during the nineteenth century. In any country the growth of consumption over the long term must be kept below the rate of growth of the real economy, so that the necessary investment can be accommodated from the national income. But on all the available statistical evidence, that has not happened recently. Astringent commentators have observed that a generation that increases the national debt in order to carry on paying itself ever-more in benefits – as Britain has done since the nineteen-sixties – is robbing future generations of the living standard that should be due to them. The Iron Law predicts these outcomes; and when it is not obeyed, economic degeneration follows.

Inevitably, the Iron Law must be suspended in time of war, when consumption of everything that is needed to wage war greatly exceeds investment spending. After the waste and destruction that inevitably occurs in a war a follower of the Iron law would demand that each affected country must concentrate absolutely on laying down productive investment, as Germany did after 1947. But in effect, in the UK, the wartime suspension of the Iron Law was continued, by a government that tried to dispense non-existent 'fruits of victory' to the people – as Britain did in 1945-50 and subsequently. No plan to strengthen a nation's long-term competitiveness in the global market can possibly succeed unless it is concordant with the Iron Law. But even in 2012 Britain's 'investment' – the government's estimate of the accretion of both productive and non-productive capital within the UK – was only 13.5% of GDP, barely half the global average and vastly less than that in the emergent economies. Germany's unique position in Europe owes everything to the fact that it has broadly conformed to the Iron Law. No foreigner should expect the German electorate to throw away the perceived advantage that the sacrifice and concentrated hard work of the post-war generations has earned for them.

The United Kingdom provided rising living standards over the whole period from 1950 to 2008, while it defied the Iron Law. The cost of this achievement was massive de-industrialisation, as investment in the material economy was avoided so that the preponderance of the nation's turnover could be given to consumption. In addition to the availability of benefits for the unemployed the Tory government in the early nineteen-seventies offered temporary family income supplements to working households as an inducement to them not to seek full compensation for price rises by getting increased wages. In the deep recession caused by the radical policies introduced by the Thatcher government in the early 'eighties the income supplements were further developed. Living standards for the less affluent employed workers have borne the brunt of the retrenchment that has been imposed on the public sector, especially since 2010, even with income credits in place. There is much talk of turning back the tidal increase in the cost of benefits and income supplements to the worst-off people in society; many of whom are employed. The explanation for the maintenance of living standards for most of the UK population [even as it has been increased by immigration and a higher birth rate since 2001] is that a Malthusian rent has been collected from national inventiveness and disbursed in benefits and tax credits. The increase in the *ik* component of consumption has been funded not by export earnings, as happened in the eighteenth and nineteenth centuries, but by taxing the revenues received by the owners of the *ik* that is embedded in the quons. The sale of profitable and promising British firms to foreigners, and the subsequent return of their profits to the new owners means that the tax-bearing capability of the British economy has massively been reduced. This intractable problem became very painfully apparent in the later years of the 2010 coalition government when the government's borrowing exceeded all planned targets because of the political requirement that both the employed and the unemployed poor should retain the minimal living standard to which they had been reduced.

Closely related to the Iron Law is the vital need fully to recognise the differentiation of *productive* from *unproductive labour*. In the most-advanced postindustrial countries most of the low-paid mass workforce in the service sector is not adding any investment to augment the *ik* or the material capital resources that are available to the economy. Only those workers who serve inward tourism and those who work as support staff in the creative sectors, along with the reviled finance sector, make significant contributions to the balance of payments. The majority of the nation participate in generating the endemic balance-of-payments deficit; with no countervailing benefit. Efficient retail distribution makes goods available to support the minority of the population who are the materially productive labour force and the creators of invisible exports or generators of *ik*, and only to that extent retail trade is indirectly productive. Retailing is becoming more efficient; productivity computed on a wage-versus-turnover basis is increasing with on-line shopping and the proliferation of discounters. But this is inescapably leading to a decline in the turnover and the corporate 'value' of the well-established supermarket chains. It is significant that the most successful new-wave retailers in Europe are built on a German model of organic growth funded by the founding family.

Many professional people and their support staff are service-providers to material industry; others support the maintenance, defence and development of *ik*: and to that extent they are highly productive. The massive health sector could be deemed productive insofar as it underpins a productive workforce; but most of their patients are not enabled to be productive in the existing economic conditions where productive jobs are not available for them on their recovery, and the increasing mass of elderly survivors are not envisaged as a productive resource

The problems of the postindustrial economies can be resolved only after their politicians and Political Economists properly distinguish productive from unproductive labour and encourage investment that supports productive labour. The idea that Economists have pushed since 1950, that a general encouragement of 'demand' will drive higher consumption which will call forth an increase in investment, has proved nugatory. Most attempts to stimulate growth have resulted in an increase in non-productive consumption, supported by a surge of imports and the consequent ruinous trade deficit, while the monetary stimulus is absorbed in a round of second-hand-house price increases. Over the coming decades a growing proportion of the unproductive majority of the population must be steered towards productive opportunities. There must be no doubt about the absurdity of a government trying to apply financial pressure to hundreds of thousands of individuals to make them pass from a category of 'unemployed' to a classification as 'employed'; heedless of whether or not that gives them access to productive work. More and more of the situations that debauched governments call 'employment' and 'apprenticeship' can only exist under state subsidy; and much of the recently-trumpeted growth in UK employment is in retailing where old-established stores face increasing competitive pressure and share with the discounters a short-term need for staff who work 'flexibly' for very low weekly wages. Most politicians' verbiage about job creation masks the reality of continuing to give handouts to paupers [i.e. the poor who are dependent on the state] who full well know that any 'jobs' or 'training' that they are compelled to undertake are sham.

# CHAPTER SIX

# POLITICAL ECONOMY AND SOCIETY

"We always have the poor with us" is a statement of fact that occurs in the Jewish and Christian bibles. It was much quoted in the many centuries when poverty and pauperism were simply accepted as part of the natural order. Poverty, squalor, starvation and disease were recognised as inescapable evils that are endemic to society, and the history of private charity stretches back to the earliest records of civilisation. Successful governments in the ancient world introduced policies to mitigate the impact of poverty, but none pretended that they could 'abolish' it. Pharaohnic Egypt established granaries to collect surplus crops in years of plenty and hold the food available for years of famine; and perhaps the most famous example is imperial Rome's frankly recognised policy to provide bread and circuses to keep the *plebs* quiescent and let the slaves do the work. In the absence of such systems of social security, the state has always been prepared to use whatever degree of force seems to be necessary, to suppress revolt and to maintain the social and economic order that enables the regime and its beneficiaries to survive. On many occasions governments have initiated aggressive wars as a means of focussing attention away from internal problems; at a high risk of catastrophic economic losses. But whenever the economy can be required to support a pattern of handouts and subsidies that keeps the unemployed and the underemployed quiescent, it has been accepted as the least painful means of maintaining the *status quo*: and that remains the case in Europe and North America now.

In this context many private sector firms have found themselves unable to fund wage increases that would match retail price inflation, or to maintain the necessary level of investment, because of the demands that the tax-and-benefits system make on their revenues. Many firms have been forced into liquidation by these pressures while their competitors in emergent countries do not have to face such large social charges. Margaret Thatcher's government was quite spectacularly reckless in replacing mass productive employment with mass benefits for the unemployed, while they also paid income supplements to hundreds of thousands of employed people. Millions of long-term benefit dependents in postindustrial countries are below pensionable age. These people have consistently been told that their means to purchase things and experiences are limited because they are 'deprived' and/or 'excluded' and/or 'disadvantaged'; and millions of benefit dependents have become conditioned simply to acquiesce in these assertions. In approving a succession of term-limited income support packages, the United States Congress has attempted to prevent the emergence of a cohort of hereditary benefit dependents. Many tens of millions of the US population nevertheless became dependent on government programmes for income support, including food vouchers; and/or on Medicaid, and/or on subsidies for 'project' housing. In the long run of economically good years between 1992 and 2007, a focus on *workfare* was broadly successful in getting millions of these people into employment. In that period the US Administration paid no more attention than did its European counterparts to the new jobs being productive of circulating capital. The unemployed were provided with training, if needed; and a short-term supplement to a trainee wage was available. The massive infrastructure spending by the first Obama Administration worked well in achieving pristine keynesian pump-priming so that the main stream of the economy was growing strongly by the beginning of 2013; and with that began a renaissance of several segments of industry that had been in decline before the recession. The coincidence of rising wages in the more advanced emergent countries with lower expectations in the USA made investment even in some marcom-making factories in the USA worthwhile

In the global context more North and South American and Asian quons will compete successfully with European brands worldwide; and they will even present increasing challenges to indigenous brands inside the EU. If imports were allowed more freely, the resulting loss of demand for output from European brandowners would further reduce the return on *ik* that has largely funded the flow of taxes into Europe's pensions, medical insurance, family income supplementation and benefits systems for decades. The cost of maintaining the reserve army of beneficiaries who are younger than pensionable age has forced up taxes on those who are able to remain independently active in the economy. For the foreseeable future almost all the EU governments will be under increasing pressure to stem the rising cost of benefits. Most beneficiaries' living standards will continue to fall, probably assisted by the device of not raising payments in line with inflation of basic prices; while strenuous efforts will be made to narrow the criteria for eligibility for benefits. Unless the fashion in policymaking can fundamentally be changed under the cold searchlight of Political Economy [which would lead to concentration on the creation and conservation of circulating capital] the tax burden on surviving firms in the already-post-industrial countries will be increased, making their products and services less competitive globally

Social immobility within declining regions will continue to harden, and sensations of deprivation will become more pervasive as the restriction of consumption by individuals is intensified. The welfare state did not 'abolish poverty', as was claimed by naïve baby-boomer politicians: poverty was masked by a plethora of unsustainable benefits that governments funded largely by borrowing and by allowing the banks to profit by accelerating the velocity of circulation to fund consumer credit. Now that the delusion of universal welfare has evaporated many young people, including graduates, face unemployment; and the relatively lucky ones find only jobs that fund a very modest lifestyle. Increased taxes will add to prices, which may accelerate the decline of more people into total dependency while many more vigorous and highly-motivated individuals immigrate from countries to the south; Asians and Africans into Europe and 'Latinos' into North Americas.

Yet still in many emergent countries a significant tranche of the population occupies a customary social status that determines, or attaches to, the individual's economic function. These include chieftainship, landholding, peasant farming, hunting, fishing, religious leadership, handicraft, or domestic service [which is often a form of slavery]. These people's consumption of home-grown and home-made commodities is supplemented by marcoms that are supplied by local craftsmen such as blacksmiths. Millions of people involuntarily occupy such a customary status by inheritance. In some legal systems such people enjoy rights of land tenure, and/or access to woodlands and waterways; or have customary rights to ply a trade. Every year tens of thousands of traditional roles are swept away in the process of urbanisation and through the industrialisation of forestry, agriculture and fisheries. Although it is very rarely recognised clearly, either by the victims or the perpetrators, forcible evictions of people from the sites that they have occupied under customary tenure deprives them of irreplaceable but undefined and unprotected *ik*; for example when smallholdings and farm buildings, workshops and homes where craftsmen marketed their own wares disappear when marcoms serving the same purpose are mass-produced. National income accounting does not include the negative impact of the huge loss of *ik* that is entailed in these processes, nor do economic planners take cognisance of the potential leverage that would be achieved if the people could deploy their inherited *ik* [including their real estate] as security for borrowing that could fund their autonomous participation in economic development. These manifestations of ignorance again display the bankruptcy of policies that are informed by Economists.

In circumstances where there is no benefit system, the people who are deprived of their ancestral assets and livelihoods in the emergent economies must seek wage-paying employment in mining, quarrying, agriculture, materials processing and transport; from which they become market consumers. Their spending generates additional employment opportunity in bars, cafés, clubs, cinemas, shops, passenger transport, communications, police, personal services, medical services, education and administration. Cash wages in emergent economies in marcom-producing plant and in service activities were of the order of 5% of a typical European nominal wage rate at median 2006 exchange rates, but that was sufficient to enable an individual to experience an acceptable lifestyle according to local criteria. Money-wages and real wages are both increasing in China and in several other leading emergent economies, and the differentiation between living standards in the postindustrial countries from those in developing economies will quickly be erased: partially by migration of people from the lower-wage to the higher-wage lands. The rapidly shifting balance of global economic power will now accelerate the changes to which this section has drawn attention.

## Personal Finance and Economic Reality

Making the transition from a traditional status within an under-developed economy into autonomous consumerism within a market economy is a stressful experience. To accommodate to such an environmental shift successfully the individual must appreciate that the more significant she or he can become as a buyer of goods and of services, and as an owner of assets [including keynic investments], the greater is the impact of that individual's decisions on the structure and dynamism of the economy in which he or she is a component. The individual must also learn that whenever people and firms opt to improve their apparent situation by borrowing, they expose themselves increasingly to the risks that attach to being in debt. Appropriate systems of taxation and regulation, and responsible access to regulated borrowing, optimally empower individuals and businesses to expand their turnover and thus contribute to the growth of an economy. However, empowerment is all too often inhibited by many factors that are endemic in both developing economies and in declining economies, including:

- excessive taxes on modest incomes and/or on purchases of mass-consumption quons, neoquons and marcoms,
- oppressive regulation causes companies to locate plant to other [less intrusive] jurisdictions, and it demoralises small business venturers; thus it is inimical to long term employment because it inhibits investment for growth,
- inadequate education in childhood, and insufficient appropriate training and opportunities for learning throughout life,
- lack of information and understanding about opportunities for enterprise, investment and for employment,
- absence of, or a lack of confidence in, institutions for facilitating saving, investment and borrowing,
- the 'poverty trap' [most obvious in some postindustrial countries]: the disincentive effect by which acquiring small savings, or gaining a pay increase at work, or accumulating even a tiny personal pension, denies a person access to benefits, to tax credits or to tax concessions
- restrictions on migrating to regions or countries where the leap to the enjoyment of a higher income level can be achieved by geographic relocation..

For the overwhelming majority of individuals in every socio-economic classifi-cation, all over the world, current quonic consumption – gratification derived from products and services that are fashionable, which embody protected *ik* - provides more certain satisfaction than does any right to receive deferred income [or any other contingent benefit] in the future. It requires great self-discipline and reason-able confidence in the stability of the economic order, combined with positive indicators of the individual's prospects for longevity, for a person *voluntarily* to forego up to twenty per cent of possible consumption in every week all through a working life of around forty years to buy a pension that may never be drawn. A desperately bad example has here again been set by the UK, where successive gov-ernments' policies since 1990 have massively reduced both the nominal and the real future purchasing power of contributory pensions that are due to become pay-able over the next few decades. There is equally little incentive for an individual to allocate a further slice of income to buy contingent keyns, such as critical illness insurance and home contents insurance, that the buyer hopes never to call upon. While the monetarist [aka neo-keynesian] delusion prevailed, millions of individu-als in Europe and North America offset the immediate impact of their surrender of spending power to tax and to pension contributions [and in the US to medical in-surance] by progressively increasing their consumer debt. The gambling instinct in humanity plays a significant and subtle part in the human consumer's calculation of wealth optimisation. Millions of people hope to be able to meet future spending requirements – and to settle their debts - from windfall gains; though they have no practicable idea how this good fortune would be achieved [and the home owners among them have already factored-in their 'equity' in the property as security for loans that they have received]. The decision by the 2010 British coalition govern-ment to allow people to spend their accumulated 'pension-pot' on retirement, rather than buy an income-for-life annuity, will provide millions potentially with such 'windfall gains', which they will always over-estimate in anticipation as they accumulate debts for resolution when they become eligible to liquidate their pen-sion funds. Thus there is a huge danger that in 'freeing' pension-savers from the obligation to buy their own retirement incomes, the number of long-living aged poor will add a burden to the government's benefits budget.

Reluctant partial recognition of the redundancy of the welfare state paradigm has created immense challenges to society and to politics. Western European states, most obviously, have supported and regulated health care, pensions and benefits systems for their peoples ever since the USA imposed 'democracy' follow-ing the defeat of indigenous fascism in 1944-5. For two generations a statistical fog of neokeynesian data and Economists' analysis enabled governments to presume that Europe was intrinsically so rich, and was possessed of such massive economic momentum, that there could never be a problem in maintaining the population at the standard of living to which it had been accustomed. It is still widely assumed that economic conditions will enable the vast majority of Europeans aged between 22 and 62 to get and keep jobs that will enable them to enjoy [at least] pre-2008 living standards indefinitely. It is also assumed that citizens will be supported comfortably by state benefits in all the cases where their earned incomes do not match their families' assessed 'needs' until they reach the age at which they will receive a state pension that funds a comfortable and varied lifestyle.

European citizens in general are not sufficiently being prepared to face the fact that the parameters within which the government can function will have to be based on the classical principles of Political Economy: expanded by recognition of the crucial role of *ik* in the economic structure. All the delusions of free-market Economics, and the consequential anomalies that the Economists chose not to notice, must separately be identified and corrected. This can be done: Britain faced the unpalatable truth in determining the Poor Law reform of 1834, when the body politic [then comprising no women and fewer than 20% of men] recognised the unsustainability of the false economy in which the receipt of personal remuneration had been separated from the individual's obligation to participate in wealth generation and to accept full parental responsibility. It will be difficult for the mass electorate in Europe and in North America to grasp this point in this century, and to accept the policies that it will dictate. During the 2012 General Election in the United States some cynics argued that there is already an inbuilt majority to be provided by benefit dependents who will always vote to keep their benefits. The alternative to radical reform is increasingly abject mass misery as the failing economy becomes incapable of bearing more taxation; while the declining number of the surviving rich retreat to the gated communities from which they deploy their wealth to exercise disproportionate leverage on political institutions.

At the great turning points of history, as in classical drama, *hubris* is followed by *nemesis* with cataclysmic suddenness: that is the way of the world. For the eurozone and the UK, and for the USA, the 'credit crunch' of 2006-8 and its immediate consequences will in retrospect be seen as the prelude to the traumatic re-education in economic reality that is yet to be experienced. The long drawn out *catharsis* is still beyond the horizon: and it is not yet possible to predict the manner in which the political structures that facilitated the economic crisis will be reconfigured.

In the period from 1873 to 1882 Britain experienced an unprecedented economic downturn. Prices, especially of crops, declined massively; and Britain's markets abroad for manufactured goods, which had been developing since the first days of industrialisation, began to decline precipitously in the face of American and European competition. Meanwhile imports to Britain of technically sophisticated products from other countries – most notably the USA, Germany and France – increased. Prices of British goods fell, and imports became more costly as they were substituted for less-advanced British products. A Royal Commission was established to investigate this situation, and the cross-party inter-professional group decided that the fundamentals of economic policy and performance must radically be changed. Thus came about the '*climacteric of the eighteen seventies*', a total reconstruction of the relationship between the public and private sectors based on recognition that the UK was no longer the predominant leading industrial power.

In general, the plans for regeneration worked, and by 1890, in a much more competitive world, Britain reached a new higher-than-ever level of prosperity; living standards also rose to a level previously not seen. In the immediate future from now Britain and most of her eurozone neighbours – perhaps even Germany, whose growth has faltered – will have to recognise a new climacteric; and to build a genuinely new strategy for the real economy, and have the guts and the will to carry it through.

# CHAPTER SEVEN

# PAST AND FUTURE

Adam Smith was just one of the millions who saw over the millennia that governments engage in competitive actions – including wars – that destroy rather than enhance their people's wealth; and that they often allow specific interests to dictate policies that are disadvantageous to the majority of the subjects of the state. So he looked for an alternative, and when he hit upon the idea of universal free trade he was so pleased with this concept that he elevated it into a principle of nature, which he imagined was comparable with the physical laws that Isaac Newton had set out. Unlike Newton's laws, Smith had no substantial evidence that his proposition brought the random data that he had collected into a coherent pattern because there were no experiments by which it could be tested and no examples that could be measured. The whole history of humanity before 1776 provided no example of free trade in operation: but Smith asserted that his principle must be correct, simply because everything else that had been tried was wrong. Almost 250 years later Economists cling to the principle, despite a continuing dearth of supporting evidence. Their 'profession' has become more monolithically dogmatic in proclaiming the benefits that the concepts of 'efficient markets' and competition would deliver if they were implemented more completely, despite the accumulating evidence that this nostrum simply did not work.

For the same 250 years democratic politicians have paid lip-service to Smith's 'great principle', but in most countries they have continued to act pragmatically: viz, to ignore it. Painful experience teaches even the dimmest of them that if they expose their people and the trades and industries on which they depend to unrestricted competition from more efficient alien firms, without allowing indigenous firms sufficient time and support to invest sufficiently to compete effectively, the home producers fail and a portion of the national income [and the jobs that it supports] is removed. Politicians must proceed pragmatically in so regulating the operations of the economy that they protect the interests of the people whom they purport to serve; insofar as they understand such interests. This chapter offers a brief review of the issues that governments and their citizens must confront in the immediate future.

## Managing Money

The last vestige of objective control of the world's money supply was lost by all the states that were members of the International Monetary Fund in 1971 when the USA abandoned the fixed gold exchange rate for the dollar. This removed from the system the last residue of the gold standard against which currencies had been measured for many centuries; and it meant that the IMF's unit of account, the US dollar, was just a *fiat* paper currency like all the others. Within each state [or monetary union] the administration of the monetary system is entrusted to a central bank: the US Fed, the Bank of England and the European Central Bank are examples of such authorities. From the foundation of the IMF until 1971 member states that deployed 'keynesian' policies to expand spending in their economies faced the prospect that if the expansion of their money supply was considered excessive, traders and speculators in the foreign exchange market offered less of other currencies for units of the oversupplied currency. If a central bank [in cahoots with the government, in each case] failed to take measures to restore their exchange rate [the traded price of their currency] quickly, the IMF would demand that appropriate action was taken. If the monetary authority could not, or chose not to, restore their exchange rate [e.g. reducing money supply, increasing taxes, cutting state spending and raising interest rates] the IMF would require that country should formally to 'devalue' the currency. This was a declaration, agreed with the IMF, that each unit of the national currency was officially to be exchanged for a reduced sum in US dollars; and by the same percentage terms of all the other IMF currencies. Thus the UK pound fell from \$4.00 to \$2.8 by 1950, then in 1968 from \$2.8 to \$2.4. By 1971 the dangers that were inherent in the expansionary economic policies that were characterised as keynesian were being asserted by some Economists, who warned that a dangerous inflationary spiral had appeared in the countries that were most tolerant of credit creation by banks and other financial institutions. Calling themselves monetarists – because they believed that control of the money supply was of greater importance than was commonly recognised by other Economists – they proposed setting limits on the expansion of the money supply to match the reported rate of growth if transactions in the economy. The ongoing increase in prices of goods and services in all the advanced countries that arose from the spread of branding and the rising component of *ik* in prices was massively compounded by the increase in oil taxes that was imposed by the governments of petroleum-exporting countries in 1973. The oil-importing economically 'advanced' countries had passed the point where the dependency of transport systems, power generation, plastics manufacture and space heating on oil was irreversible: so rising costs spread through industry and commerce, and in response labour unions demanded higher wages and they became increasingly aggressive whenever the spiralling increase in wages and prices twisted against them.

In the later nineteen-seventies governments talked tough about resisting the inflationary pressure – which impinged on most aspects of public spending and most sources of taxation – but they remained anxious to maintain momentum in their economies, so they would not compel the banks [and related institutions, such as building societies] to terminate their creation of credit and their lending. Provided that the rate of increase of **M** [money supply] did not exceed that of **PT** [the naively computed national income] the system was considered to be under control. From 1978 to 2006 Monetarist policy – according to that simplistic formulation – was considered to be a success. That was an illusion. It was shown in earlier chapters of this book that increased borrowing was made possible for consumers and for firms by various new and revamped tricks such as securitisation which increased **V** [the speed with which purchasing power flows around the economy]. Thus consumption focussed on brands [of which an increasing proportion were imported, especially to the UK and the USA] was facilitated, enabling alien brandowners to draw larger profits to fund accelerated expansion of their exports. Also facilitated by the uncontrolled increase in **V** was an increasing inflation of house prices which enabled the owners to feel asset-rich as their 'equity' in their homes increased. Thus households were enabled to increase their debt-to-earnings ratio to maintain or increase their range of consumption of quons and quonic experiences like holidays abroad. For thirty years successive governments and central bank governors [in the case of the UK, from 1978 to 2008] maintained the charade of monetarist rigour while they largely ignored the mode, pace and extent of the growth of lending. The fact that Monetarism [as it was implemented] had been nonsense was exposed progressively from early in 2006 to the late summer of 2008 when arose the prospect of a collapse of all banks due to their interdependent lending to each other.

At the height of the crisis in 2008 the Fed and the Bank of England, followed by other central banks, first enabled some of the stronger banks to take over failing banks and finance houses and then supplied the newly merged or nationalised firms with the means to maintain payments of their combined obligations. Once the immediate crisis that threatened the existence of banks had been overcome, the central banks created cash with which they bought assets from the licenced banks, thus replenishing the banks' purchasing-power sufficiently to enable them to settle obligations as they fell due. In simple terms, the credit that had been created by financial firms expanding the velocity of circulation was replaced by volumetric credit. Governments and Bank Governors hoped that this inflation of the recognised money supply [quaintly called *quantitative easing*; QE] would enable banks to continue lending to firms in the 'real economy' so that output could be maintained. In the event, especially in the UK and several other EU countries, lending by the banks to the supply-side of the system was restricted because revamped regulators forced banks to accumulate much higher reserves that were seen as the means by which a repetition of the 2008 crisis can be avoided.

Most of the American assets that were bought under the initial phase of QE by the Fed, and virtually all those bought by the Bank of England, were state securities [government bonds, and bonds issued with a guarantee from the state]. Thus in the process of maintaining the liquidity of the banks the central banks became the owners of a significant portion of the national debt. Only later did the Fed and others buy tranches of commercial bonds to continue with 'recapitalising' the banks. A remarkable feature of this process was the fact that most of the 'bad' loans that banks had saddled themselves with came from reckless extensions of traditional forms of lending, especially in the residential and commercial property sectors. The notional 'value' of property that had been funded by the increased velocity of circulation that was facilitated by securitisation was unsustainable; but nobody knew by what quantum the 'unperforming' portfolios of homes, hotels and shopping malls would ultimately be reduced if the organisations that owned these assets could be allowed to continue in existence. Thus a very slow process of portfolio rationalisation, with disposals of some of the more attractive assets, was begun in 2009 and by 2012 many areas of the markets had been stabilised [in some cases with reduced 'valuations' but in others, as with top-drawer London residential property, the prices went up]. Similarly in the UK and other areas of the EU the banks extended loans that they had made to 'zombie companies' so that these unperforming assets could be disposed of advantageously if the economy made a sufficient recovery.

By contrast with traditional types of loans, the vast majority of innovative bets, notably derivatives, futures and swaps, remained credible throughout the crisis period. The reconstituted banks demonstrated that they could best build up their reserves through making profits in their gambling business. This perception was very unwelcome to the Economists and politicians who failed to see how the impact of a high **V** had mocked Monetarism, while enabling this solidly-based arena of transactions to be developed. In a huge display of ignorance Economists, most politicians and many commentators condemned 'casino banking' out of hand. They lacked the common sense and the intellectual flexibility to recognise the simple fact that speculative wholesale gambling can be economically useful and profitable: given that it cannot too often be stressed that it should be managed, regulated and financed separately from mainstream retail and wholesale banking.

The size of the US economy in proportion to the amount of QE that was released by the Fed reduced the risk that the process would trigger significant retail price inflation, and a modest increase in inflation was anyhow considered to be acceptable as a stimulus to growth in the real economy. In terms of Fisher's Law, in the USA an increase of **M** is most likely to stimulate the expansion of **T** while bank regulators would [in due course] try to prevent an excessive increase in **V** by raising interest rates. At the time of writing central interest rates were kept at rock-bottom, but if this strategy succeeds when the economy expands strongly the relatively small price impact of the monetary expansion would be accepted as beneficial by participants in the real economy. In the UK, by contrast, increasing **M** beyond the process of QA would most likely facilitate an increase in **P**, while the bankers stimulated more turbulence by increasing **V**. For several years from 2010 there was a rapid increase in London house prices; which could not simply be explained by the extraneous factor that multi-million pound houses were under very high demand from cash purchasers from overseas: all classes of property in London increased quickly in price. The overwhelming majority of more modest properties were bought by ordinary British residents, who were prepared to take on larger mortgage *kos* in reasonable confidence that they would be able to sustain them from their income or to settle the debt on an advantageous sale of the property. The government provided underpinning finance for mortgage lenders for middle-of-the-range homes, and the lenders themselves avoided [for a time] reckless loans such as had become common before 2007. The demand for homes, especially in the south-east of England, was so extreme that people made sacrificial commitments to get on the 'housing ladder' [often assisted by family members] and the price of a modest dwelling in London increased in 2012-14 by a 'value' that exceeded the total average annual wage of British employees.

The Bank of England expects ultimately to report a profit from holding assets that have been purchased under QE. It could use that fund as a reserve with which to underwrite a properly structured and regulated wholesale betting market. London could consolidate the role that it developed between 1987 and 2007 and has largely retained. If Britain does not take this massive fortuitous opportunity to develop an effectively regulated, adequately reserved, globally accessible megabetting business – which the world palpably wants to have available - the time-lagged consequence of QE in the shrunken UK economy would be highly disruptive general inflation. If the UK fails to risk-manage the after-effects of QE constructively and opportunistically, the whole economy will experience inflation.

The International Monetary Fund [IMF] was set up alongside the United Nations in 1945 with the hope that it would serve as a world central bank; but the Soviet Union soon withdrew from the new institutions and took its satellites with it. Thereafter for more than thirty years the IMF was effectively an economic wing of the NATO/SEATO system of alliances, to which Germany and Japan were admitted after their rehabilitation. India and other former colonies joined the IMF on gaining national sovereignty. Under the original set of rules the exchange rates for all the member currencies were quoted in US dollars, and devaluations or revaluations of currencies against the dollar were subject to approval by the Fund. This worked until the US dropped the gold-exchange standard in 1971. Soon after that the IMF created its own unit of account and reserve currency, SDRs: Special Drawing Rights. This made for a confusion of roles: the IMF was partly a regulator, partly a bank, partly a research institute and partly a talking-shop. Following the collapse of the USSR the ex-communist countries eventually joined the club, as did China. The changing pattern of world trade and the increasing wealth of the emergent economies forced the IMF constantly to change the proportions of its reserves that related to each of the major global currencies; and the valuation of Special Drawing Rights was set by reference to a regularly revised 'basket' of the national currencies. The initial dominance of the wartime allies was perforce replaced by a more realistic allocation of votes in the Fund between countries, according to their presumed economic strength.

The Bank for International Settlements [BIS] based in Switzerland, was established after the First World War as a clearing-house where the central banks could make settlements between themselves and lend money to each other behind the veil of Swiss banking secrecy. Because the BIS members are generally-like-minded central bankers [sometimes ex-politicians, but explicitly acting as bankers and not as political representatives] they were able to reach agreements that would have been much more difficult in the highly politicised relatively open sessions of the IMF board. Thus it was the shadowy BIS that set guidelines for how much capital banks should hold as a proportion of their total capital and in relation to the amount that they lent to others. Since the noughties' crunch, governments and central banks have required banks under their governance to adopt the constantly evolving 'Basle Rules' promulgated the BIS as the primary prudential requirements.

World leaders will eventually be led to a new consensus on how to develop a global financial system that can properly serve 'real' trade and industry, and regulate the appropriate use of speculative bets. Such a system must serve the transcendent interests of humanity and not be riven by national interests. The long-suppressed need for a global monetary standard which could form a basis for global liquidity could be met by Keynes's original proposal for an **M** to be issued and controlled by the International Monetary Fund, *bancor*. With an upgraded constitution and a balance of voting power that in real time reflects the contemporary pattern of world economic strength, the IMF could allocate access to reserves of bancor to each country [or monetary union], proportional to the trade and gross national product of that currency area. Money is too important to leave to the individual control of national governments: that is why the gold standard survived for so long, and why that concept has adherents even today. Clarity in the operation of Fisher's Law, and in verifying the balance of payments for each monetary area, can be optimised by using bancor, and until that is achieved instability and gamesmanship will be inherent in the system of international trade and in every facet of global monetary manipulation.

## Globalism

The defence of *ik* and the management of revenue arising from its possession, and not any principle of 'free trade', predominates in the evolving global trading nexus and in the growth of both personal and national wealth. It is in the reciprocal interests of states that they all protect intellectual property. In the nineteen-forties corporations based in the USA consolidated their control of a high proportion of the world's leading brands, and seventy years on that country probably has an even greater predominance over the rest of the world in brands that incorporate income-generating patented and/or copyright *ik*. These facts have hitherto enabled the post-cold-war superpower to sustain a massive medium-term deficit in its federal budget and on its trade in 'goods', most notably with China and with oil exporters.

By the start of the second decade of the twenty-first century the rising living standard of an increasing proportion of the workers in China pushed up wage costs; and that in turn led Chinese firms to concentrate more on making components for their own indigenous brands that aimed to capture the growing home market for quons, diverting the primary focus from marcom exports. As Chinese real wages increased, the prices of some marcomic components from China rose sufficiently that it became viable for some firms in the USA to begin, or to resume, or to expand their own marcom production on US territory. The American industrial renaissance can be expected to strengthen and eventually there will be expanding markets for wholly US-manufactured quons – including US-made components - in China, India and Brazil as living standards rise there. The countries that have funded the emergence of their manufacturing sectors largely by exporting marcoms to the postindustrial world will increasingly become mixed economies in the dual sense of providing a quon-based lifestyle for an increasing proportion of their home population while having a sensibly pragmatic approach to the retention and development of significant public sector services in the fields of health and education.

The majority of Americans continued to enjoy one of the highest living standards in the world in the years after the credit crunch. The exchange rate of the US dollar declined, greatly helped by quantitative easing and in consequence of the accumulation of an ever-greater public debt. The negative signs for the future that these data predicate do not alter the fact that the recognised strength of the US economy ensures that securities issued by American banks and US public sector debt remain acceptable to be held as reserves by private and public institutions all over the world. The credibility of those debts depends on the continuing ability of American firms and US government research facilities to develop their *ik* ahead of overseas competitors. A huge risk to America's predominance will arise as the government makes further reductions in the space programme and in defence research, both of which have supplied massive intellectual resources for civilian applications. The United States' economic hegemony, which has underpinned its dominant political position since 1943, can progressively be eroded in the coming decades if China and other emergent economies develop their own military and space research and exploit the *ik* derived from spin-off technologies while the US and the EU continue with the policy of disengagement from investment in military and naval capability. But just for now the US retains a very significant technological advantage: while China, as the most massive creditor to the US Treasury in history, has a vested interest in the stability and credibility of the US debt

It has been noted that between the nineteen-sixties and 'nineties the peripheral countries in the European Union forfeited sectors of high technology by eliminating an array of small specialist businesses when the member states 'rationalised' the large-scale smokestack industries for which the small firms had provided technical support and specialist inputs. Before the cull large old steelworks and factories were conspicuous for a high output of pollutants and high maintenance costs. They were also paying tightly-unionised labour very high wages [by comparison with earlier periods and with other countries] to make marcoms that could be more cheaply produced by more modern plant - and in many cases by primitive workshops - in low-wage societies. This industrial change was accompanied by a major cutback in the demand for coal and the consequential redundancy of miners. The modernisation of transport networks led to a great reduction in the workforce on the railways as most shunting of coal and goods wagons was eliminated, single-manning of trains became common and vastly fewer signalmen were required; while computers enabled operations to become quicker and more efficient. The mass unions that had been able largely to dictate terms of employment that set norms for the whole workforce lost most of that power; so while highly-skilled Europeans continued to have higher wages than the global average into the twenty-first century an increasing proportion of employees faced static or even declining real wages as their employers faced increasing global competition. Much of what Germans continued to value as the *Mittelstand* – freestanding, innovative, entrepreneurial small and medium firms – was eradicated in less far-sighted countries. Between 1980 and 2010, as the number of the nonemployed throughout the postindustrial world increased: with a peak in 2009-10, so the bill for benefits, for pensions, for student support and for bureaucracy increased. This demand for cash to pass through government accounts led both to increased taxation [on everybody, but especially on the employed and on their employers] and to burgeoning government debt. Year by year more of the state's increasing turnover was allocated to the non-employed; and much of that monetary flow passed on as consumer spending from European beneficiaries to exporters in the emergent economies. Unlike the UK, however, most continental countries in the EU retained the manufacturing of locally popular brands: so while low-value-added manufacturing declined, brandowning firms with relatively high productivity [reported in terms of revenue gained per euro spent] remained viable.

Under the delusion that any 'inward investment' must be 'a good thing' successive UK governments had no qualms about firms being sold to aliens together with their brands and their portfolios of *ik*. Politicians preferred to ignore the massive difference between alienating *ik* together with surrendering the subsequent income flow accruing to it, and the importation of foreign capital to support the development and expansion of firms that remain indigenous to the country. In many cases where *ik* is alienated, at first the new owners were happy to continue running obsolescent plant in the UK as long as the net profit that they could make from global sales of the brand was satisfactory. But as the plant became more costly to maintain, especially if the wages payable in the UK remained disproportionately high compared to pay rates in emergent countries, factories are closed. Some localised products [such as Harris Tweed, Stilton cheese and Scotch whisky] continue of necessity to be manufactured in the United Kingdom; but more and more of the material components of the alienated British brands that were successful on the world market were no longer British-made. Successful business operations produce circulating capital that the owners can deploy wherever it best serves their global business plan. A large proportion of foreign-owned but British-registered firms retained some research and development functions in the UK because of the combination of experience, expertise and invention that was available to keep their *ik* refreshed and competitive. Some innovative British firms have secured the ownership of highly-demanded *ik* that captured a global market, and remain British-owned. But many innovative companies that were capable of rapid growth were unsupported by bank loans or by venture capital sourced within the UK, and so their frustrated owners sold their interest on terms that compensated them personally for surrendering significant potential future earnings. Foreign-owned firms that sold British-branded quons were not incentivised to repatriate manufacturing to the UK even when the cost advantage of manufacturing in China was reduced; it was most advantageous for firms to locate their next mass production facility in whichever low-wage economy offered the highest probability of holding down costs for a sufficient run of years to ensure that the plant paid for itself.

Italy retained a whole raft of significant indigenously-owned firms which sold strongly branded quons made in Italian factories. The French politico-economic elite moved easily between the civil service and the finance sector, and they ensured [with little need for explicit direction by the government of the day] that key companies and essential basic technologies were kept in French ownership or sealed within euro-companies; if necessary with large-scale recapitalisation organised by the leading banks and insurers, which were themselves kept in French ownership by the same means. Major infrastructure including railways and electricity supply remained under state control and although alien investors [and would-be investors] in the private sector railed at the restrictive measures that preserved jobs at high wages for relatively short daily working hours they could not crack the consensual France-first approach.

Leading firms in the emergent economies plan in the medium term to sell branded quons around the world. Their governments do not want to impede those firms' accumulation of capital, or to choke off the growth of the home market for their emergent brands, by enabling the minority of relatively wealthy consumers to get too deeply into a habit of buying alien-branded quons. The exceptions to this principle are the franchised distribution of global brands of ephemeral quons, particularly software and access routes to the internet, fashion clothing and accessories, beauty/grooming products, news and information and social media, tobacco, drinks and fast foods. These imports occur illicitly when they are banned; so most governments permit - and tax - controlled quantities of these imports; to keep the higher earners content within the country, where they invest and provide innovative leadership. Larger-scale sales of foreign-brand quons may be permitted as national wealth rises, especially where the material components of the quons are assembled [and preferably sourced] and distributed by the local partner in a joint venture. Similar constraints apply to importing capital equipment and profes-sional services: the medium-term net benefit of the import must be demonstrated before foreign exchange is released for the purchase. During the past fifteen years in China and in India, and in a score of other emergent economies, a quantum leap in marketed economic activity has been supported by the rapid and [with a few notable lapses] well-managed development of protected markets in indigenous wholesale and retail keyns. Foreign expertise is encouraged to set up 'representa-tive offices' in most of these countries, to inform the development process; but aliens are not usually given traders' licenses on terms that would enable them to forestall or to eclipse indigenous start-up providers of marcoms, of quons and of services including the management and issuance of keyns.

The ongoing rise of the emergent economies will quickly enable their citizens to buy hundreds of billions of quons and neoquons every year, whose makers will pay little or no tribute to American or to European owners of *ik*. Over the next dec-ade established international brands will come under much more intensive competition than they have yet experienced, especially from the emergent Asiatic and Latin American brands. New brands constantly improve their competitiveness by combining lowest-cost manufacturing with globally sourced *ik*; including the physical design of the product and of its packaging; and it would be very unwise to ignore key examples of global diversity like Australasians' transformation of the wine industry - even in France - or the phenomenal achievements of Australia, New Zealand and South Africa in sports and medical science. It would also be foolish to ignore the possibility of European firms taking advantage of cheaper labour and the continuing fecundity of entrepreneurial ability to create new facilities for pro-ducing marcoms as well as to develop new quons.

Corporations and sovereign funds that are based in the most rapidly emergent economies - and in countries that control globally significant supplies of oil, gas and scarce minerals - will increasingly often be encouraged by their governments and their national monetary authorities to buy the ownership of firms that control significant American and European brands, including buying control of keyn-trad-ing corporations and their brands. The extent to which public sector US debt is owned by foreign governments and central banks might eventually force the US to be less restrictive in allowing the ownership of US brands to be alienated. There is a real risk that at some time and for some time American stockholders will sell con-trol of corporations to pay down the burden of debt on the public finances; and this would change the balance of power in the world economy. The new alien owners of the established brands would be able largely to repatriate the net earnings that could be generated by the *ik* that they have bought, relocating productive invest-ment from post-industrial to new-industrial economies. In an increasing proportion of instances the new owners' scientists and technicians located in their home coun-tries take over the next-stage development of the *ik* and its applications. Japanese firms that offshored a massive proportion of their manufacturing twenty and more years ago are now becoming concerned about their country's declining percentage share of the turnover from global trade; they will press their financial institutions to fund major new technologies, as well as to exchange passive holdings of US securities for active control of a wider range of viable global brands.

On the other hand, facing election every two years, members of the US House of Representatives are acutely aware of the need to convince their constituents that they will enact measures to support fair trade and reciprocity with other nations, especially when US employment is threatened by low-priced imports or by alien attempts to take control of US corporations. This results in temporary bans on, or limitation of, or penal taxation of certain imports; and to more permanent protectionist measures such as a veto on some companies being taken over by foreigners. Measures are also enacted to ensure that US interests retain full control of productive capacity in strategically sensitive areas. Similarly, exporters from other continents must charge significantly higher prices for many categories of the quons and neoquons that they sell in the European Union than they charge in the rest of the world, to meet the requirements of Europe's 'anti-dumping' regulations. Specific controls on a relatively limited range of cheap imports have also been applied in Australia and the other advanced countries which have been subject to the onslaught of the new manufacturers.

The most successful products from emerging countries will soon be marketed globally as fully-fledged brands alongside the Korean brands that have become established in Europe and North America. Products to which middle-income consumers and pensioners in postindustrial countries have become accustomed at neoquon prices will be improved and rebranded as quons; consequently many of the old-world consumers whose purchases have helped the new-world producers to invest in creating the new brands will no longer be able to afford them. To maintain an approximation to their existing pattern of consumption, less affluent consumers in the importer countries will be compelled to settle for the next wave of neoquons; some of which will be of inferior quality because of the lower technological level that will initially be achieved by the next cohort of firms based in the newest emergent economies from which retail stores in the postindustrial countries will source their most price-competitive own-brand neoquons. Alongside this development, indigenous brandowners will construct [or rescue] plant in which to undertake production of input marcoms, and of the final product and so partially re-industrialise the postindustrial world.

A very significant shift in the distribution of the world's increasing wealth between states and economic communities is now well advanced. Driven by investment, the balance of power is very obviously moving from the original OECD countries towards the wide range of emergent economies that experience forward surges of development and market success, interspersed with setbacks which frequently result from changing conditions in their target markets. Any attempt to inhibit relative decline within any of the postindustrial economies by imposing import controls would reduce the accessibility of products to consumers; especially the availability of neoquons to the beneficiaries of state-provided incomes and subsidies.

## *Diversity within Globalism*

Since the financial crisis peaked in 2008 most governments have been compelled to abandon the delusion that they have ever-expanding capacity to borrow a higher proportion of the national income in successive years. Especially in the postindustrial economies politicians have to surrender the unrealistic hope that future national income will automatically become sufficient to service their accrued public debts while providing more welfare for more dependents year by year. But, even now, few policymakers have had sufficient mental preparation to recognise that it is an unacceptable political risk to offer people a 'right' to incomes, or to income supplements, that cannot be assured in the future.

In the early twenty-first century, following the remarkable recovery and reorientation of China, the realignment of India alongside the USA after the collapse of the USSR, and the limited opening of access for foreigners to financial services in major Latin American states, development planners aspire nowadays to achieve the *simultaneous* emergence of mass marcom production [including crops and livestock], and brand recognition of indigenous quons. To generate funds to assist the development process several emergent economies provide highly marked-up quonic services in information technology [using their abundant educated human resources] and provide luxury holidays for affluent alien visitors; while facilitating a significant export of people. Quonic services that are provided for visiting foreigners range from conducting pharmaceutical trials, outsourcing IT services, working in brothels and acting as guides on safari, to providing hospitals for 'health tourists' who undergo complex or ethically challenged procedures at a fraction of the price they would have to pay in their home countries. A private hospital will only attract international customers next year if it provides satisfactorily quonic levels of service to its current patients, so the treatment and the ambience for recuperation must be quality-controlled to the best international standards. Motor racing and other spectacles have been promoted just as well in Malaysia as in France; and, in one notorious year, Grand Prix provision was much better in China than in Britain. While the Chinese built their Olympic stadiums, India became dominant in commercial cricket; and the success of the *Bollywood* film industry is legendary. Thus it was demonstrated even before the end of the last millennium that international tourism, media, call centres, sport and leisure can contribute significantly to the turnover that generates investment to fund economic development. Modernisation need not be spread over three or more successive human generations of mass industrial drudgery. Increasingly, individuals can be intellectually and psychologically prepared for participation in rapid change. With access to intercontinental media via the internet, they can fill gaps in their knowledge and understanding without risking the loss of face that can so easily inhibit individuals from asking or answering direct questions of people close to them. The development programme for an emergent economy demands massive imports of expertise and of quonic plant; and huge investment in the economic infrastructure, including banking, education and communications.

Some naïve commentators have confused the price impact of proportionately increasing consumption of quons in China with 'inflation'. The basket-of-goods that a middle-income employed Chinese buys is increasing in price year-on-year for three main reasons: one is that a significant element of monetary inflation is systemic in a rapidly-growing economy, and China has generally managed this aspect confidently and competently [despite repeated western predictions that it would fall apart in a crisis]. The second is that some commodities are becoming dearer in the long term, due to global economic factors which China is trying to address by investing in primary production in African [and other] countries. Meanwhile the third, and increasingly the biggest component in rising living costs, is that Chinese consumers are able each year to replace marcoms with quons, and to have wholly new quonic consumer experiences: one of the most significant of which is to occupy an urban apartment. The biggest risk to stability in the development of China is generally recognised as the risk of a collapse of an unprecedented boom in property development that has been financed by increasingly-adventurous 'shadow banking'. The risk that some of the least-regulated lenders might collapse, or be found to be fraudulently managed, expands with the volume of total lending that the sector supports and the extent to which property prices exceed the cost of building the units.

Once more than five per cent of the consumers in an emergent economy can afford to consume a mix of indigenous and globally branded quons, that cohort becomes dominant in shaping changes in the demand pattern for the entire economy. Taxes and import controls can continue to constrain the growth of demand for some imported brands, encouraging sales of emergent local quons. Around twenty per cent of the population of China, of Brazil, of India, and of several other significant emergent countries, has now entered into a lifestyle that is becoming broadly comparable to that of their peers in the more advanced economies; and many millions more have a consumer experience that includes increasing access to locally franchised global quons and significant use of indigenous brands. Upwardly mobile consumers recognise the catalytic role of innovators in providing them with jobs and with opportunities for self-employment, and they perceive the counter-productivity of doctrinaire socialist opposition to the emergence of private affluence provided it works together with state-dominated banks in driving forward investment.

The government of China accepts the prospect of half a billion people consolidating their quon consumer status, and at least another fifty million becoming higher spenders, in the shortest possible timeframe; so that their country can move on from the residual legacy of the slave economy that the Mao regime imposed. Already many millions of individuals throughout China have reinvented themselves in the roles of cash-crop market gardeners, or as fish or poultry or pork farmers, as restaurateurs, as traders, or as components manufacturers or commodity processors; and their example is available for others to adopt. The farmers join skilled urban workers in expecting to consume quons: so the prices of agricultural commodities necessarily rise for that reason, ahead of global price movements, and in addition to meeting the costs of intensification of farming in terms of water, energy, fertilisers, and genetically modified or 'organically' certificated seeds. The flourishing of small businesses is a fundamental sign of economic health and dynamism. It was a feature of economic structures in Europe at least since the sixteenth century; but that is now under threat from taxation, the rise of regulation and the unavailability of finance for investment: Asia generally has not yet fallen into that trap.

India under its radically new government is renewing the challenge to enable hundreds of millions of people consciously to shift themselves from traditional to consumer status and to provide a more effective economic infrastructure for the hundreds of millions who are already consuming quons, and to allow the sixty to seventy million top earners to secure their superior lifestyle and more confidently to accept entrepreneurial, technical and managerial responsibility for the transformation process. Wilful traditional inertia has hitherto characterised much of the Indian population, as was repeatedly manifest in riots against development schemes; and it was a feature of much of the rhetoric that marked the celebration of sixty years of sovereignty in 2007. A large number of Indians from a range of ethnic and religious backgrounds have declared a clear preference to remain in their traditional rural and caste condition; declining to integrate dynamically with the global economy, which makes the economic management of their subcontinent an area of very special interest in the coming period. The immensity of corruption in politics and under a bureaucracy that is inherited both from the British Raj and from the subsequent neocommunist regime has also been a huge barrier to efficient economic development throughout India.

Demand supported by this evolving pattern of consumer preferences will enable firms in the rationally governed and [relatively] corruption-free emergent economies to develop their brands and prepare them for global distribution; without suffering the drain of capital that is lost in the postindustrial countries to high taxation. Some emergent economies will also continue to export people to the other emergent economies and to the postindustrial countries, where some of them compensate for local skills deficiencies. Other migrants to the postindustrial countries take low-paid jobs and so help to keep wage rates for the unskilled indigenous workforce in check; or even force wages down, which has over recent decades made it even more favourable for some natives to opt for benefits rather than employment. The migrants' remittances to dependents, and their savings returned to their countries of origin, drain away circulating capital to support the balance of payments and promote investment and economic growth in their homelands.

Africans are migrating in a tidal flood to Europe. In the recent past many have managed quickly to qualify as state beneficiaries, especially those who were allowed legally to settle in soft-touch countries like the UK; but that is likely to change. More importantly, the legal migration of many of the better educated and more ambitious African individuals to take up careers in Europe intensifies the self-inflicted tragedy of post-colonial decay to which much of Africa has become prey. Many of these migrants have fled from kleptocratic governments which allow terrorists, gangsters and warlords to prevent coherent economic development. The progressively more abject despoliation of large tracts of Africa by Africans has been tolerated by the global community for two generations; but now the continuing chaos in some countries is obviously obstructing access to sources of energy, crops and minerals that are needed by the emergent powers.

Global corporations avoid investing in countries where the decaying colonial-era streets are unsafe, regulation is ineffectual, deadly disease is rampant and the officials are corrupt; and these issues are exacerbated where violent religious fundamentalism emerges. Where highly priced natural resources occur in an unstable country's territory whose exploitation is considered essential by an international corporation, the facilities that they construct are protected by imported security services. Thus a new form of armed economic imperialism has emerged, as is seen in some oilfields and mining, quarrying and agricultural areas. Many other potential sources of significant wealth remain undeveloped – or have been abandoned – because of the absence of effective law and order and the prohibitive cost of guarding and insuring the facilities and those who work there. For so long as both indigenous intellectuals and international *grauniadistas* continue to shield the reality of politicians' brutal incompetence behind a smokescreen of anti-colonialist hypocrisy, much of the African continent will show itself to be incapable of self-help or of optimising natives' benefit from assistance from outside.

Polynesians migrate to the Americas and to Australia or New Zealand; and people from Caribbean islands settle in North America and Europe. Millions of *Latinos* are reclaiming their collateral ancestors' lost territory: unnoticed for who they are by white and black US citizens who classify as 'Hispanic' millions of people whose genetic inheritance is predominantly 'Native American'. The global migratory pressure is not yet bringing a significant flow of migrants [other than from even less-successful former Soviet Republics] into Russia; and chauvinist Japan allows little more than time-limited work permits for skilled individuals in the finance and media sectors, alongside a significant traffic in housemaids and sex workers; consequently both those countries face a 'crisis' of diminishing population. Islamic countries whose governments have attempted to remain open to the mainstream of globalisation are increasingly under pressure from more militant exponents of the religion; and in territories where militant Islamists have succeeded in undermining public order – or have seized power overtly – interaction with non-Islamic trade and industry is at best uneasy and sometimes becomes impossible.

In recent decades several postindustrial countries have received significant net immigration of culturally alien immigrants, some groups of whom are virulently racist or religiously assertive against the host population. Some EU governments have promised to admit only skilled or wealthy individuals from outside the Union, who can reasonably be expected to pay taxes as required. Machine politicians carefully avoid acknowledging that their class has granted citizenship or resident status to millions of assertively unassimilated immigrants; while they recognise that the resulting problem is not simply one of numbers. The total number of immigrants who have no expectation of becoming assimilated is still increasing in consequence of the continuing import of spouses and of other relatives who will reinforce their community's linguistic, sartorial and institutional alienation from their hosts; and their high fertility, compared to the indigenous population, compounds this issue. Hundreds of state-funded immigration lawyers demand that the state should provide benefits - including free legal aid and priority housing - for new arrivals, some of whom are coached in the specious rhetoric of 'human rights' and are briefed to declare that they would expect to be tortured if they returned home.

'Human rights' were first formulated as an idealistic aspiration, but the outcome in several of the countries where the concept has been enshrined in law is that the opportunity to freeload on the system been exploited. Ever-widening judicial interpretations of ill-drafted statutes have served as licences for lawyers to precipitate an exponential expansion of contested hearings and appeals that taxpayers have been compelled to fund. 'Human rights' are also the spurious basis for endless interventions and delays in the process of criminal justice, especially under the English adversarial system by which lawyers tie up police time and enable witnesses to be lost, or intimidated, or [by lapse of time] to become unreliable in their recollections. Until control of the situation is recaptured from them [ideally by terminating the adversarial system altogether] Britain's increasing over-supply of litigators will continue ruthlessly to develop their specious human rights business; and the cost of the whole charade threatens to spiral out of control. As an increasing proportion of the indigenous population shows itself to be open to racist right-wing propaganda which has drawn on these facts, mainstream politicians have begun to make tentative concessions to those who are demanding an end to 'multiculturalism'.

Global cross-border trade in fake pharmaceuticals and illegal drugs, in slaves, in armaments and related technology, has grown massively since 1990; and the human rights industry has fostered, rather than hindered, these sinister developments. The international black economy is now markedly more significant than it was in any earlier era. By their nature these activities are not quantified in any country's official statistics: thus their role in accelerating globalisation and changing the pace and pattern of economic development through illicit flows of circulating capital cannot be assessed with any accuracy. Counter-terrorist and anti-money-laundering measures may slightly inhibit the further development of these crimes; but the rewards are so great, proportional to the alternative lifestyle opportunities that are open to the operatives, that evasions of state procedures will continue on an immense scale.

## Current Opportunities and Challenges

As the world's economies become more and more interdependent there proceeds the often ruthless destruction of traditional assets and environments. These events include removing peasants from their land, closing shoreline fishing bases to make way for beach bars; demolishing small temples, stalls and workshops, bakeries and laundries on sites that are designated for urban redevelopment; and denial of tribal groups' right to preserve a forest in which to hunt. Even in areas where environmental derogation is moderated due to fears about global warming or recognising the economic opportunity of preserving rare environments for tourist development, the destruction of customary lifestyles will continue. At the close of the eighteenth century the English poet, John Clare, was driven mad under the strain of his unusually profound awareness of the deprivation that he experienced when the fields and woods and common land of his native village were enclosed in large fields to produce cash crops for distant urban markets. Clare first described, then – after it had gone forever – he tried in every detail to recall the way of life and the landscape as they had been before such a fundamental change deprived the members of the peasant community of their customary autonomy.

In a profound misconstruction of this phase of development, some Economists have recently picked on 'commons' to present a model of 'perfect competition' superimposed on an idealised vision of feudal society. If common land could be fairly accessed by all members of a village community on equal terms, they would all have the opportunity to benefit equally from it. But if someone commandeers a disproportionate share of access to the land, or of resources on the common, that disproportionate individual gain is loss to everyone else. In reality no open market idyll like that which is assumed in the model ever existed. When a common existed in association with virtually every village in feudal Europe, the lords managed the commons as part of their estates. Usually acting through a reeve or steward, the lord determined which land he would have under his own direct management, and which the peasants were entitled to use for grazing their animals and for firewood collection and berry-gathering. The surname Hayward perpetuates the memory of the trusted senior villager who allocated access to the grass on the common as a source of winter cattle feed. With rare exceptions, English common rights were extinguished when the land in the village was allocated to freeholders [including the lord] under an Enclosure Act. At the other end of Europe, Russian serfs frequently reminded their lords, 'we belong to you, but the land belongs to us'; and that remained true from Catherine the Great's consolidation of serfdom until the serfs were emancipated by Tsar Alexander II. At the emancipation the Russian lords were awarded ownership of some of the land, in compensation for their loss of ownership of the serfs. The freed peasants were required to make 'redemption payments' to their dispossessed masters to secure their share of the land, which were only completed in 1917: the year of the revolution that was to strip them of all their assets.

In power, the communists quickly expropriated the owners of the 'means of production, distribution and exchange', including land tenure of all kinds and independent professional practices. They intended to eradicate the aristocracy as well as the capitalists; and these brutally naive expropriators of tangible assets ignored *ik*, except where foreigners could be made to pay for use of copyright material that was generated by Soviet subjects. Very different transformation strategies have been adopted in China and in the former Soviet Union since the failure of the Leninist project became palpable. The processes of economic evolution that have been taking place in Russia and in China over the past two decades have unsurprisingly produced very different reactions among the population. Despite the very real progress that was been seen from when Putin first became President until the 2014 confrontation with Ukraine and the imposition of western sanctions, Russia still festers with resentment of a tiny cohort of beneficiaries of corrupt 'privatisation', and there is widespread popular incomprehension at the ability of a 'mafia' of chancers to continue to bend circumstances to their own advantage Meanwhile China permits any politically conformist individual to emerge as an affluent role model, which indicates that there is an opportunity for others to emulate them. Continuing corruption in the public administration of both huge countries is an admitted issue, of incalculable extent: to which no comprehensive solution is yet proffered.

Global brands can emerge from any country, under almost any regime. Leading brands like *Fiat, Sony*, and *Boeing* have proved their resilience; and ownership of brands can be bought and sold by corporations based in other countries, as *Volkswagen* owns the fully rehabilitated *Skoda* brand and *Ford* sold *Jaguar* and *Land Rover* to *Tata*. A Canadian corporation that owns a globally distributed brand of Scotch whisky can have its advertising designed in France and invoice its customers from a service centre in India. Scandinavian furniture makers locate their factories around the world in relation to the cost of transporting their products to the consumer: then they repatriate the returns on *ik* that form a significant component of the prices of their quons. Services and supplies can be bought wherever the brandowner can find the best combination of cost control and requisite quality of marcomic inputs to a final product; and the work can be switched to alternative suppliers at the end of every contract period.

Despite globalisation and the trend towards consolidation of major companies, niche and local brands will continue to thrive all over the world; driven by dynamic or obsessive people. Some such firms are linked to the tourist trade, some serve the specific requirements of sects or cater for people with fads or disabilities or hormonal imbalances, and many pander to the super-rich. Many highly-differentiated consumer groups can now find each other by internet and are thus freed from a need for geographical proximity in sharing access to less common consumer experiences. Several governments find this consumerist 'open world' threatening to their hegemony. A ruthlessly oppressive regime can very largely prevent any significant access to internet shopping by its subjects; but anywhere where a neo-democratic rule of law prevails the demand of individuals to be able to allocate their own resources as they wish cannot be suppressed entirely.

So long as the system of states and 'communities' of states continues, the crucial economic questions that are only rarely asked by governments or by firms, or by consumers or by the electorate [but almost never by Economists] include the following:

- what proportion of the world's protected *ik* is domiciled in this country, in total, and by economic sector?
- where does this country stand in this league with other countries?
- how *effectively* is *ik* that is claimed by this country's native firms and individuals protected by patent, copyright, brand, trademark etc. In how much of the world is that protection enforced? What trends or shocks are likely to affect the effectiveness of the defence of that *ik* ?
- what is the level of resilience of this country's domiciliary *ik* in the face of a major shift in demand away from the products or service categories to which that *ik* contributes?
- are firms and research institutes in this country investing enough in designing, testing and protecting the next generation of *ik*? How is this assessed and evaluated?
- are this country's tax and regulatory regimes optimally conductive to the generation, exploitation and defence of robust *ik* by our citizens and residents? If not, what is being done, by whom, to improve the situation? How will their success be verified?
- what proportion of the world's *ka* trade is conducted in this country's currency?
- is the international *ka* trade that uses this country's currency genuinely profitable to this country [i.e. producing a net balance of payments surplus over a short run of years]?
- what proportion of the *ka* trade that is undertaken within and through institutions in this country is 'genuine finance' and what proportion is gambling contracts? Do the regulatory systems and tax regimes properly take account of, and enforce, this differentiation; and of the total quantum of trade that is involved?
- What is this country's balance of payments on insurance services?
- what proportion of world *ka* trade – denominated in all currencies - uses contracts that are framed [and, if necessary, enforced, arbitrated and/or litigated] in this country's legal and/or regulatory system? To what extent are the related legal services beneficial to the balance of payments?
- what proportion of the international *ka* trade that passes through this country do indigenous firms and individuals own? What proportion do organisations and individuals based in other countries handle? In each case, what proportion is 'genuine' finance and what proportion is gambling?
- what net contribution does international finance make to this country's *per capita* income; and how does this compare with other countries?

- what is this country's balance of payments [net] between all fees, dividends and tribute paid to foreign owners of assets located in this country, vis-à-vis all fees, dividends and tribute paid by persons and businesses outside this country to economic agents domiciled in this country?
- how strong and how speedy are the measures by which Ponzi borrowers are identified, with lenders compelled to withdraw from any such position?
- what net contribution do and can properly-defined gambling activities make to this country's national income and to its balance of payments; including activities that have been characterised as 'hedging' or 'casino banking' and what additional products or methods are yet to be implemented?
- what degree of risk to the stability of the currency and the financial institutions is derived from the country's exposure to 'genuine' international financial trade passing through its firms and institutions?
- what degree of risk to the stability of the currency and to the balance of payments is presented by international gambling contracts that are regulated and contractually due for settlement in this country?
- what proportion of the economy's quon sales is of brands owned by indigenous individuals and corporations?
- what proportion of the sourcing of the components used in assembling indigenous brands [*ik* and material inputs and labour] occurs within this country's territory, including coastal waters and directly-ruled overseas territories?
- what percentage of the cost of native quonic products is expended on imports of components [including materials and foreign-owned *ik*]?
- what is the potential of this economy to maintain or improve its position in manufacturing/assembling material and immaterial quons?
- what is this country's balance of payments for shipping services and air transport, including sales and purchases of vessels and aircraft?
- what proportion of this economy belongs to resident tax-payers; both as individuals and as shareholders/bondholders in institutions [including the state's share of ownership]?
- what access to indigenous raw materials, or what climatic conditions, or other geographical factors give this country [or economic community] comparative advantage or disadvantage [vis-à-vis other economies] that can materially affect its situation within the global economy?
- what is the balance of payments for this country, between the tribute that foreign owners of *ik* and of material assets [e.g. land, utilities and factories] receive from this country, as against the tribute that foreign economic agents pay to this country's indigenous owners of *ik* and of material assets?

Crucial questions by which a Political Economist can assess the resilience of demand in a country or an economic community include these:

- What proportion of the adult population autonomously generates household incomes that are deemed not to require any supplementation in doles, credits or benefits?
- What is the spread and distribution of *per capita* income within this group?
- What proportion of taxation do they bear?
- What proportion of public services do they receive?
- What proportion of saving do they contribute?
- How effectively are their savings directed into potentially productive investment?
- What is the probability per cent of these people losing their relatively secure status?
- What proportion of today's independently higher-paid individuals could ultimately move through middle income status to existence as beneficiaries; over what timescales?
- What proportion of the adult population earns household incomes that provide a middle range lifestyle; which may attract some means-tested benefit?
- What proportion of this group could reasonably be deemed to be in whole or in part *productive* employment?
- What proportion of the national product that is estimated to come from this group is reasonably assessed to be productive [i.e. replacing the costs of its production and contributing to investment in future production]?
- What is the *per capita* expenditure stratification of this group?
- What proportion of taxation do they bear?
- What proportion of public services do they receive?
- What proportion of their incomes do they contribute to savings?
- How effectively are their savings directed into investment?
- What proportion of taxation do they receive as benefits?
- What proportion of them is employed in the public sector?
- What is the stratification of state employees within this category, in terms of the proportion of their income that is received as tax credits, child allowances etc?
- What is the probability per cent of people from this category achieving high-earner status within one, three and five years?
- What is the probability per cent of the middle income receivers descending over what timescale into benefit dependency?
- What proportion of the adult population is predominantly or wholly dependent on benefits?
- What are the *per capita* income levels of any sub-categories that the state

has designated within this cohort, and how do these compare with incomes received as median middle-range incomes?

- What is the rate of increase or decline of the beneficiary proportion of the population?
- What proportion of total taxation do the beneficiaries bear?
- What proportion of all taxation do beneficiaries receive as benefits? At what rate is this increasing or diminishing?
- What is the probability per cent of the elevation of persons from this category to unsupported earner status, over what timescale?
- What, if any, contribution does this category make [overtly, and illicitly] to current production and to investment in the future capability of the economy?
- What, if any, statistically significant proportion of the population has traditional economic status [tribesmen, priests, etc]?
- What is the aggregate size and the present impact of the existence of this subset of the population on the economy?
- What are the probabilities of any of these groups entering more fully into the market economy as producers, and how would that shift impact on existing projections and plans for the economy?
- What, if any, contribution do the various segments of this category make to investment in the future capability of the economy in their present condition?

These data would enable pragmatic economic planning to be undertaken, in line with our updated tenets of Political Economy, even accepting that many of the early results may be wide estimates. Only a genuinely productive economy can provide good public education, comprehensive health care, secure defence, and fair pensions and benefits for a significant proportion of its population. The universal operation of Goodhart's Law means that if any of the answers to the long list of questions that has been set out above is elevated to form a template for economic management [including manipulation of the monetary system], it will cease itself to be acceptably accurate.

Prevailing policies in most of the formerly-industrial countries militate against the sort of optimisation that could be achieved by devising the policy agenda in line with the data that will be disclosed in the answers to the questions that are set out above. Immediately after the threatened meltdown of their market in 2008, the surviving financial institutions were cautious in securitising debt bundles for resale. But since 2009 state-assured terrestrial purchasing power has been made more abundant to the banking system than it had ever been before; yet banks have largely ignored requests and admonitions to make more credit available for investment by smaller corporate borrowers. Financial institutions were required to increase their reserve ratios: this they did by hoarding cash and by reducing their exposure in the form of risky loans.

A saving grace for some postindustrial economies is that for the next decade, maybe two, the emergent economies will continue to need to licence access to western **ik** and to buy high-technology plant from the USA and Europe; and they will be keen to maintain access for their exports to markets in postindustrial countries. The emergent global brandowners will also continue to conduct their trade with other parts of the world – both commodity purchases and sales of marcoms and of quons – in terms of the established reserve currencies for which the central banks in the postindustrial economies are responsible. So the Russian, Asian and Latin American central banks will selectively support the dollar, the yen, the euro and even sterling to facilitate their increasing influence on global trade; during an extended period in which the continuing availability of retail debt in the postindustrial countries will enable consumers to continue buying energy from Russia, Arabia and the Gulf, Africa and Latin America.

*Levin's Law* states that bankers are so impenetrably purblind and arrogant that they will plunge headlong towards a new crisis as soon as the last one has been resolved for them at the expense of the taxpayers; and after much distress to innocent individuals. After the next 'crunch' or 'crash', sovereign investment funds from the emergent economies will only participate in again recapitalising western banks if the funds' owners then reckon that they still need the western firms; and the terms of any participation will tip the scales of world economic power even further away from Wall Street and the City of London.

# CONCLUSION

The massive human tragedy that followed the imposition of Marxist regimes in Europe and in much of Asia provided a depressing example of how idealist theory can become a curse upon humankind. Within a century [1917 to 1991] the Leninist application of Marxism failed, not least because it incorporated an irrational repudiation both of the acquisitive instincts of human beings and the fact of the existence of *ik*.

It has been seen that normative Economics was invented in the eighteen-sixties, partly as an attempt to refute Marx's ideas, but principally to develop a form of 'economic science' that was derived from the pure stem of Adam Smith's dogma. Often called the 'marginalist' or 'Austrian' school of Economists, the founders simply set aside the scientific laws of Political Economy as they were then taught and which were generally accepted as well-evidenced axioms for statecraft. The Economists imagined how economic events - transactions - could be maximised by perfectly efficient firms trading with 'rational' customers in a completely apolitical economic space. Their model assumed that all the disembodied participants in their economy would equally be empowered to acquire all relevant information that would enable them to take the best possible decisions on which to determine economic events. That model has never resembled the world of flesh and blood, of human psychology, of political reality, of sophisticated betting [as on derivatives] or of material production and consumption. The Economists ignored the fact that free trade has never been implemented; they simply asserted that their extreme model should be taken up in everyday life.

In the nineteenth century the much-trumpeted free trade principle was set aside whenever the fact that "trade followed the flag" justified imperialism: which Adam Smith quite specifically abhorred. There was no prospect of cross-frontier free trade being implemented for Britain or France until their empires had formally been abandoned. Today, in direct conflict with pure Economic theory, the mass electorate in the advanced countries consistently supports domestic policies that seek to control the allocation of wealth through society in the face of the much-trumpeted fact that [in the states where politicians are under the tutelage of Economists] inequality of income and of wealth is increasing. Yet in the real world regulations limit what products may lawfully be made, what level of taxation is imposed on different commodities and services, what ingredients may be used, where processes may take place, what emissions are permissible; and what steps must be taken to prevent environmental damage or detriment to human beings as employees, or as users of products or as members of the general public. In the formerly communist countries the professors spout both Marxism and Marginalism while the capitalists and the fixers obey the laws of the jungle. In the countries where politics has been to a greater or lesser extent in thrall to Economics, living standards were reduced dramatically for millions of citizens in Greece, Cyprus, Spain, Portugal and Ireland after 2008; and millions more were less seriously impacted in Italy, France and the United Kingdom. Policies that were devised and/or sanctioned by Economists since 1950 have diminished productiveness, have justified deindustrialisation, have concealed inflation whenever significant increments of credit are slid into the housing market, and have sanctioned mass dependency on benefits which necessitated the accumulation of unsustainable levels of public debt.

Recent climatic traumas and extreme weather events have emphasised the fact that there is a very dynamic tension between the basic material demands of consumers [for water, air, energy and food] and the limits of the world's capacity to provide them in a sustainable environment. It is feasible for a population whose fecundity is rationally controlled to enjoy a rising standard of living and to apply the necessary resources to counteract changing global conditions. Individuals can be empowered to gain access to the fruits that arise from the constantly increasing *ik* that their species can generate, employ and adapt. Understanding and acting on these simple Malthusian principles is the golden key for securing the future comfort and concord of humanity.

After the credit crunch many efficient European and American firms continued to generate abundant circulating capital, much of which was seized as taxation that was increasingly dissipated in unproductive consumption. The residue of the profit remained in the hands of established companies and many of them hoarded it, paralysed by fear that any investment may fail in the prevailing economic circumstances. By contrast, most notably in the UK, start-up companies that developed new concepts addressed to new markets – even the many that could display evidence of success - hesitated to seek loans to fund their growth because the company's owners were likely to be subjected to excessive burdens [even risking repossession of their homes] if the business should fail to service the loan.

It is plainly in the interests of *ik* owners worldwide for their countries to adhere to fair-trade agreements, most-favoured-nation treaties, agreements to recognise each other's' *ik* and other reciprocating asset-protection measures that have misleadingly been categorised as 'free trade' arrangements. They are all essentially managed-trade deals that protect the micro-monopolies on which most of the protection of intellectual property depends. *ik* is the primary generator of profit and thus of circulating capital; and 2013 was significant as the first year in which more money was spent by major corporations in defending their *ik* than in seeking to extend it by research. The productiveness of labour is highest where the employees are skilled, confident and in good health: bodily and psychologically. The output of slave labour – including forced or fake jobs imposed upon the unemployed - is generally inferior in both quality and quantity to that from free labour.

One of the most-cited quotations from Keynes's *General Theory* is that:

"Practical men, who believe themselves to be exempt from any intellectual influences, are usually the slaves of some defunct economist. Madmen in authority, who hear voices in the air, are distilling their frenzy from some academic scribbler of a few years back."

The quotation has frequently – and most unjustly – been turned against Keynes himself, as scribblers of the present era try to apportion the blame for the economic crisis that recently engulfed the postindustrial world. Keynes was in no way responsible for the 'keynesian' Economics that contributed so liberally to the near-fatal malaise that resulted from the excessive development of unproductive consumption funded by inflation, most completely in the UK, through most of the time since Keynes's untimely death. No previous or subsequent observer of the economy has written such well-honed tracts for the times: books, essays and other writings that exactly related the crucial data of the day to fresh thinking that was absolutely relevant. Keynes's self-appointed successors were sadly lacking in comparable abilities.

The attempt to force the economy to adopt 'rational' market behaviour, as it has been presented in Economics since the Second World War, has been ruinous. An alternative basis for understanding and managing economic life is patently needed. Some observers will think it strange that I should urge them to seek authoritative guidance from authors who were long-dead when Keynes wrote the *General Theory*. But much valid natural science derives from Archimedes, Pythagoras, Euclid, Laplace and Newton because their observations can be verified by the newest experimental and observational techniques. The challenge with which this brief text ends is to ask the reader to assess how far the long-ignored [but never disproved] laws of Political Economy – combined with a proper appreciation of *ik* - can provide a clear understanding of the massive problems that have been thrown up by the catastrophic mismanagement of the economic system since the demolition of the command economy that managed the stresses of supplying the nations and the military in World War II.

At the very heart of Britain's exemplary economic failure lies Adam Smith's assertion of the free trade principle; which was made really dangerous in 1890, when Alfred Marshall produced his *Principles of Economics*. That seminal text presented the new Economics as an exposition of how everyday business practice and consumers' actions should be understood in 'scientific' terms. In reality it was no such thing: it was mere speculation without supporting evidence. But it *looked* like a science book, with illustrations of parabolic curves and even equations. Academic Economists loved it: it enabled them and their graduates to pose as scientists. For almost a century and a half they have pushed this idea, of a norm to which reality should conform. Unsurprisingly, every time it has been 'applied', especially within a context of keynesian macro-economic policy, with which it is incompatible, the dogma has produced unfortunate results; in response to which Economists, like first-world-war generals, demanded that the policy should be pursued with increased vigour.

So why has Economics been accepted, worldwide, as a neo-science? Why are Economists tolerated now? Their favoured policies have not worked: they can never work. So what can be done?

Any country or economic community can depute its bureaucrats and academics to work honestly through the list of questions that is posed in this chapter, providing truthful answers – however embarrassing that may be – and assessing what can be done to improve the score that exists in their economy today. At least, and at last, the context is amenable: there is a significant measure of understanding even among politicians that *something must be done.* Stalin's notorious article under that title released a reign of terror: the will to 'do something' in the world of 2015 could have a beneficial result.

### Bancor

J M Keynes's concept of a global reserve currency. **Or** is the heraldic term for gold, and thus bancor means bank-gold. Controlled by the IMF, it would replace gold as it was used to underpin the global currency system under the pre-1914 gold standard.

### Brand

A legally recognised and protected corporate name, trade name or product name which signifies the quality and service standards of one or more **quons**.

### Circulating capital

The portion of the receipts from sales of goods or services that is available for allocation to wages, profits or new investment [after the firm has met all the costs of production, including maintenance of the plant, and all taxes and other impositions by the state and its agencies].

### Consumer's surplus

The spending power that remains to a consumer after making a purchase for which they pay less than the price of the most-preferred brand that serves the purpose for which the purchase is made.

### Cost centre

An organisational unit within a productive sequence that is resourced to perform a specified task [or group of tasks].

### Cyberkeyn ©

A financial instrument **[ka©]** that exists only in **cyberspace** [an immaterial universe occupied by electronic data] that is the subject of an enforceable contract under a specified terrestrial juridical system.

### Direct labour productivity

The estimated monetary valuation of the output that is attributable to an individual [or the average attributed output of a team] in extractive industry, manufacturing, logistics or distribution.

### Emergent economy

The economy of a state or community that has not yet achieved 'advanced' economic status.

### Ephemeral quon ©

A branded 'consumer good' or experience which is consumed in a short period: such as an entertainment experience, a drink, a session of legal advice, a meal or a journey.

### Estate

The total assets and liabilities belonging to a person or to a legal person.

### Firm

A legal person, which may be a registered part of a group of companies or agencies, or an operating division of a company, or the trading wing of a charity or association; that has been set up to perform specific economic functions.

### Good.

A 'widget', in 'neoclassical/Austrian/marginalist' Microeconomics. It approximates to a marcom ©.

### Goodhart's Law.

The idea that whenever any datum is taken as a key indicator of the state of an economy, it ceases to serve that purpose.

### Grauniadista

A British citizen of the fashionable soft left, who is likely - if salaried - to have a job that was advertised in a certain publication.

### Ik © [Intellectual keyn©]

Any intellectual property that is definable and defensible at law as an asset. [Pronounced as in 'trick' or 'quick']

### Jevon © [May be abbreviated to jev© or represented as J]

A physical object whose valuation is what a buyer will pay for it now, without reference to the cost of production of the asset. The category covers antiques, works of art and all other 'collectors' items'. [Adjective: jevonic].

### ka © [Keynic asset ©]

An asset held by an economic nucleus, that was created as a debt by [or was lawfully imposed upon] another economic nucleus.

[Pronounced as 'car' without the r]

### Keyn ©
Any financial asset or liability, or item of intellectual property.

### ko © [Keynic obligation ©]
A debt: the reciprocal of a **ka**.
[Pronounced ko as in 'cocoa']

### Legal person
Any corporate or charitable or state-controlled entity that has economic functionality and legal recognition [e.g. a 'corporation sole': a bishop in his working capacity].

### Levin's Law.
The proposition [by the columnist Bernard Levin] that bankers are so intractably arrogant and stupid that they will start working to create the next crisis as soon as they have been rescued from the effects of the last one.

### Macroeconomics
The study of the operation and management of national economies and of groups of economies that are controlled under community arrangements.

### Marcom©
A manufactured output which is sold as a physical product, in open competition with other items supplied to closely similar specification, with no warranty and not conveying to the purchaser any access to protected **ik**. Broadly the equivalent of a **'good'** in marginalist economics.

### Marque
A model or sub-brand within a brand.

### Megabetting
Sophisticated gambling, usually undertaken by firms [but with some high-networth individuals participating]: the category includes derivatives, spread bets, and most options and futures.

### Microeconomics
An academic presentation of how Menger, Walras and others in the period1860-80 supposed that markets function.

### Natural person
A human being.

### Neoquon ©
A product or service that performs the same physical function as a quon, but is sold under the brand name and/or warranty of a retail store, at a price less than the normal retail price of the quon and usually without the cachet that attaches to a brand.

### Opportunity-cost
The economic options that are surrendered when a nen or cen commits limited spending power to a purchase in preference to alternative purchases.

### Piracy [of intellectual property]
Illegal use of proprietary **ik**.

### Political Economy
The name of the multifarious attempts to set out scientifically the rules which appear to point to success in the management of a regional, national or wider community economy. It was in use from about 1540 to the end of the nineteenth century, when Economics quickly became an academic orthodoxy. In the seventeenth and eighteenth centuries Political Economy was closely associated with Mercantilism, in which the primary object was to strengthen and protect the economy of the individual state; if necessary at the cost of other economies. Between 1750 and 1820 there emerged a series of Laws and Principles that apply to any economic system. These Laws have never been disproved or refuted; merely side-lined: as a consequence of which the 'real economy' has been undermined. The Laws were set out in the context of the eighteen-seventies by Millicent Fawcett in a hugely popular textbook, *Political Economy for Beginners*. I have attempted to summarise her text and update the system in a companion volume to this one: *An Introduction to Political Economy*. An online version of Mrs Fawcett's original text is accessible at the University of California Library.

### Postindustrial [country]
An economy in which the proportion of the population engaged in manufacturing and extractive industry is less than 60% of the number of employees that were so engaged at the country's highest-ever level of such employment.

## Productiveness
The contribution of an economic process to the generation of circulating capital, to be available for investment.

## Productivity
The measurement of the process efficiency of an industrial or commercial process in terms of cash-per unit of output or of service, or the labour-hours per unit of output.

## Quon©: a quasi-jevon.
A product or service, usually branded, that gives the consumer access to protected **ik** and offers significant consumer guarantees, which is priced above the cost of materials and processes deployed in providing the material components, enabling the supplier to meet the costs of maintaining the brand's exclusivity and its reputation with its users. The price is sanctioned by the desirability of the brand to users.

{Quon is pronounced 'kwon' with a short 'o' as in 'none' or 'gone']

## Real estate
See real property

## Real property
The ownership of a specified location on the earth's surface. The current market price of any parcel of land depends on two sets of factors:

- first, the degree of security of the ownership [how firmly the proofs of ownership would stand up, if subjected to a legal challenge];
- second, what crops, structures or other assets occupy the site: what is the perceived current market price of the ownership of the plot and the existing premises [and/or mineral right, crops, amenities etc];
- third, when land is leased, the rental depends on the period of the lease and on the degree of security that the tenant is granted, and on the perceived valuation of the assets in relation to the distribution of human activities; the quonic utility of the structures or other amenities that occupy the site, and on the potential to change the use beneficially during the lease period.

The potential alternative use of the land and/or the structures on it may greatly increase or diminish the market price of a parcel of land; any significant change in derives primarily from secondary **ik**; such as gaining [or failing to gain] permission to change use.

### Rent

The term used in classical Political Economy [c1800 to 1870] to mean the 'surplus' that is received by a producer – and, in particular, an agricultural producer - over and above the material costs of production and the cost of capital [the rate of interest that would have to be paid to borrow the money necessary to acquire the plant and consumables; including the wages advanced to labour]. While Ricardo ascribed this to the 'natural and indestructible powers of the soil' Malthus hinted at the understanding that it was derived from what is described as **ik** in this text.

### Solvency

The capacity of a corporate entity or an individual to meet all legitimate demands for settlement of debts and other obligations at the due times.

### Surplus value

Marx's interpretation of circulating capital under the capitalist system, where it is all appropriated by the capitalist class for fixed investment in preference to allocating a fair proportion to raising general standards of living.

### Systemic risk

A risk that is sufficiently great that it can result in the reputational destruction or the insolvency of a corporate entity or a person.

### Transaction

An event in which an asset is bought or hired.

### Warrantied marcom©

A marcom that is sold with a retailer's [or, rarely, a wholesaler's] guarantee or warranty: a **neoquon ©**.

### End.

Printed in Poland
by Amazon Fulfillment
Poland Sp. z o.o., Wrocław